MARCO POLO

BER LIN

Mecklenburg-
Western Pomerania

Schwerin

Lower
Saxony

Brandenburg

Berlin

POLAND

Saxony-
Anhalt

Hanover

Potsdam

Magdeburg

Leipzig

den

T0106884

www.marco-polo.com

THE
TOURING APP

shows you the way...
including routes and offline maps!

GET MORE OUT OF YOUR MARCO POLO GUIDE

IT'S AS SIMPLE AS THIS

1 go.marco-polo.com/ber

2 download and discover

GO!

WORKS OFFLINE!

SYMBOLS

INSIDER TIP   Insider Tip

★   Highlight

●●●●   Best of...

☼   Scenic view

Ⓢ   Responsible travel: for ecological or fair trade aspects

(*)   Telephone numbers
that are not toll-free

**PRICE CATEGORIES
HOTELS**

Expensive   over 140 euros

Moderate   90–140 euros

Budget   under 90 euros

Prices per night for two people in a double room with
breakfast

**PRICE CATEGORIES
RESTAURANTS**

Expensive   over 25 euros

Moderate   15–25 euros

Budget   under 15 euros

Prices for an average main
course without drinks

CONTENTS

DID YOU KNOW?
For bookworms → p. 22
For film buffs → p. 24
Berlin on the water → p. 35
Time to chill → p. 44
Floating pool → p. 58
Fit in the city → p. 61
Gourmet restaurants → p. 68
Local specialities → p. 72
Spotlight on sports → p. 96
Luxury hotels → p. 102
Budgeting → p. 129
Currency converter → p. 130
Weather → p. 131

MAPS IN THE GUIDEBOOK
(138 A1) Page numbers and coordinates refer to the street atlas
(0) Site/address located off the map
Coordinates are also given for places that are not marked on the street atlas

(𝕄 A–B 2–3) refers to the removable pull-out map

INSIDE FRONT COVER:
The best Highlights

INSIDE BACK COVER:
Public transportation route map

The best MARCO POLO Insider Tips

Our top 15 Insider Tips

INSIDER TIP In memoriam

Micha Ullman's *memorial* to the Burning of the Books on Bebelplatz under the Nazi dictatorship draws our gaze downwards. Below the sheet of glass empty bookcases can be seen that symbolise the 20,000 books burned here on 10 May 1933 → **p. 31**

INSIDER TIP Cloudy forecast

Berlin's traditional breweries are dead – long live craft beer! The *Privatbrauerei am Rollberg* brews its unfiltered beer on a site formerly owned by the Kindl brewery, and you can sample their output in the neighbouring tavern → **p. 90**

INSIDER TIP Berlin from below

The tours run by *Berliner Unterwelten* will take you to forgotten locations under the streets of Berlin. Wandering through old bunkers and escape tunnels under the wall is hugely exciting, but not for the faint hearted! → **p. 56**

INSIDER TIP Fresh from the lab

The *Erfinderladen* shop specialises in quirky new inventions. For fans of neckties that come with a pocket for your schnapps bottle, or cutters that remove the crusts from your bread → **p. 80**

INSIDER TIP Stalinist glory

The 90 m/295 ft-wide *Karl-Marx-Allee* in Friedrichshain with its monumental, Moscow-style housing blocks is impressive (photo above) → **p. 37**

INSIDER TIP Paddling in the Spree

In the *Freischwimmer* restaurant and water lounge (photo right) you can enjoy the romantic location on the river bank, rent a canoe or kayak and explore the Spree. Life jackets available for children → **p. 69**

INSIDER TIP Vegan gastronomy

The brunch menu at *Kopps* proves that a vegan diet needn't be a joyless affair. To eat here is to understand why veganism is so popular in Berlin → **p. 75**

BEST OF...

FOR FREE

● *Lunchtime concerts*
From September to June, you will be able to enjoy a free lunchtime concert every Tuesday in the *Philharmonie*. The performing ensembles are first-rate and include the Berlin Philharmonic and scholarship holders from the orchestra's academy → p. 95

● *Wall art*
The *Eastside Gallery* (photo), the longest open-air gallery in the world, is located to the south of the Ostbahnhof railway station. Take a look at what artists have left for future generations on a 1,316 m (4,317 ft) long piece of the former Berlin Wall → p. 48

● *Rock for free*
Free admission on Thursdays at the *Sageclub* in the Heinrich-Heinrich-Straße underground station! Turn up before 10pm and dance for free at "Rock at Sage" → p. 90

● *Déjeuner sur l'herbe*
In summer, the Berliners pack their picnic baskets on Sundays and make a pilgrimage to the *English Garden* in Tiergarten to relax and listen to free concerts of jazz and Klezmer music. Join in the fun! → p. 41

● *Watch democracy at work... or just enjoy the view*
Walking up the glass dome of the *Reichstag* building is free, however, you have to register in advance and there are queues. Inside, down below, you can watch the German parliament at work; from the roof terrace, you have a great view over the city → p. 47

● *Under street lights*
The *Gaslaternenmuseum* ("Gas Lamp Museum") located in the Tiergarten doesn't just display historic street lights from across Europe; it's also the perfect place to take an evening stroll under romantic lighting – and it's all free of charge. The oldest exhibit is 200 years old → p. 31

❲ ❳ ❳ ● Dots in guidebook refer to "Best of..." tips

● *Quadriga with twelve legs*
The *Brandenburger Tor* is an absolute must. Not only the street artists let their hair down here, there are also many hobby photographers. Who can take the most beautiful picture of this city landmark? → p. 41

● *"TV asparagus"*
This is the name the people of Berlin have affectionately given the *Fernsehturm* on Alexanderplatz. You will really miss out on something if you don't visit the viewing platform 203 m (666 ft) above street level – it's the best view in Berlin → p. 34

● *Party in the park*
Every Sunday during the summer, the *Mauerpark* transforms into a festival site, complete with live music, karaoke and a flea market selling everything from old knives to trendy canvas bags. You can't get more Berlin than that! → p. 80

● *Queue up for your favourite Berlin food*
Cheap but tasty – that's all a Berlin currywurst needs to be, with some chips or a bread roll to go along with it. The Berliners queue up at *Curry 36* in Kreuzberg for a grilled sausage with curry powder → p. 74

● *Sophisticated shopping*
Time and time again, the *Ku'damm* has been pronounced dead, but the many customers in the fashionable boutiques on the elegant boulevard cannot all be wrong. This is where Berlin is at its most glamorous in a setting of magnificent old buildings: typical of Berlin – but sometimes beautiful can be expensive → p. 55

● *Don't forget your swimsuit...*
You will feel like you are at the seaside: deck chairs and sand as far as the eye can see. The wide expanse of water at *Wannsee* is an inviting place to sunbathe or swim, and a snack bar is never far away (photo) → p. 24

● *Jazz in a beer garden*
Real Kreuzbergers don't give a hoot about the yuppies in Mitte or Friedrichshain when they sit back with a pint in their hands in one of the beer gardens on a balmy summer evening – listening to live jazz in the popular *Yorckschlösschen*, for example → p. 94

ONLY IN

BEST OF...

● **Under water**
The sharks and crocodiles in the *Zoo-Aquarium* become especially popular when it's raining cats and dogs outside. You will find it much more peaceful upstairs among the snakes and tarantulas → p. 56

● **Cultural centre**
Fancy the Processional Way in Babylon, Caspar David Friedrich or Nefertiti? You will be really spoilt for choice trying to decide between the five museums on the *Museumsinsel* with their magnificent collections → p. 38

● **Expedition to the tropics**
You will feel like you are in a jungle in the tropical plant glasshouse in the *Botanischer Garten* it is so warm and humid among all the palms, ferns and lianas → p. 56

● **In a tent**
The tent-like roof at Potsdamer Platz is not only a protection from the rain. The *Sony Center* (photo) also offers a huge range of entertainment and culinary delights. The setting is particularly impressive in the evening when the coloured LEDs in the ceiling start to glow → p. 45

● **Shopping under cover**
A creative factory charm and original pop-up stores selling quirky accessories and fashion by Berlin designers make *Bikini Berlin,* the city's alternative department store, the perfect hang-out on bad weather days → p. 81

● **Vertical garden**
The tropical plant wall in the café at *Dussmann's* cultural department store is a fantastic setting for a break when it's raining outside. Try their delicious cakes and snacks. You can also browse around the store's massive selection of books and music media → p. 82

RAIN

RELAX AND CHILL OUT
Take it easy and spoil yourself

● Dream away
You float in salt water and listen to underwater music in a kind of grotto. The sauna, steam bath and massages in the *Liquidrom* next to the Tempodrom are pure bliss → **p. 44**

● A cup of tea
Taking part in the Chinese tea ceremony in the *Berghaus zum Osmanthussaft* calms down even the most hectic person. The world's noise simply is left outside the door → **p. 57**

● Beach bar
In summer, you can lie back in a deck chair in *Strandbar Mitte* with a view of the Spree and Bodemuseum. In the evening, join in a dance and indulge in a pizza from the wood-fired oven → **p. 89**

● Sweating Turkish style
Let yourself be pampered in true oriental fashion in the *Sultan Hamam* in Schöneberg – hamam and Turkish massages → **p. 44**

● Fairy-tale figures in the park
The water splashing out of fountains and fairy-tale figures is tremendously soothing and the fresh air performs miracles. You can regain your stamina at the *Fairytale Fountain* in the Volkspark in Friedrichshain → **p. 50**

● Pfaueninsel
This idyll on the outskirts of town is easy to reach with the BVG's double deckers and a ferry. Wide stretches of grass are the perfect place to relax or have a picnic, and peacocks roam around freely → **p. 59**

● Breath of fresh air
Tired of the big city? The best way to relax is to take a stroll around the *Tempelhofer Feld,* the site of one of the city's former airports. Watch kites flying in the skies above and let the sound of the wind drown out big city noises. It feels like being in the countryside (photo) → **p. 60**

INTRODUCTION

DISCOVER BERLIN!

Berlin attracts creative people from all over the world as if by magic and is *one of the most popular cities of the world*. No other city in Europe has as much art and culture to offer! No matter whether it is art, dance, theatre or music, the cultural scene in Berlin provides a stage for international stars and also acts as a breeding ground for talented youngsters to develop their skills and become the real avant-garde themselves. With its more than 150 concert halls, theatres and other stages, three opera houses and around 180 museums and art collections, Berlin has an enormous variety of cultural institutions.

Apart from the Museumsinsel with its magnificent exhibits, the treasures found in the more than 440 small galleries are equally unique. This has made Berlin one of the most important cities in the *art-business world*. For the people of Berlin, culture is not merely the Staatsoper and Philharmonie but also the countless concert clubs and tiny theatres "round the corner" where superb performances are often held and seats are cheap. Berlin is also famous worldwide for its *feverish nightlife* with more than 200 clubs, innumerable bars, cafés and pubs. Some places only open at midnight and stay open until the early hours of the morning – if they close at all. The "in" districts of Mitte,

Friedrichshain or Neukölln represent Berlin as it likes to think of itself: as an international metropolis.

Today, you hardly ever get the feeling that this city was *once divided by a wall*. In the past, however, you didn't need a compass to work out where the East stopped and the West began. The wall that ran through the centre of the city from 1961 to 1989 could really not be missed. In the one half there was East Berlin, the capital city of the German Democratic Republic that came under the influence of the Soviets and, in the other half, the walled-in city of West Berlin under the protection of the western allies France, Great Britain and the USA. Now, 25 years after the Fall of the Wall, visitors to the city can barely see the difference in a cityscape that once developed differently as a result of the two political systems. Many of the prefabricated concrete buildings which were typical of the GDR in the eastern part of the city have been revamped. They look so surprisingly modern and cosy that living on the 8th floor of a building on Alexanderplatz is now considered chic. And, when you stand at Checkpoint Charlie – the erstwhile Allied border crossing on Friedrichstraße – you will see that the former eastern sector is dominated by luxurious business premises and boutiques while a certain dreariness has spread across the west.

> **Despite the burden of history Berlin is growing back together again**

With a population of around 3.6 million, the new – and old – capital Berlin is still in a period of upheaval. Enormous efforts have been made since the reunification of

Unter den Linden boulevard ends at the Schlossbrücke – with the Berliner Dom in the background

Germany to create an *architecturally representative capital city*. There are continuous building, restoration and revitalisation activities everywhere. After the demolition of the Palast der Republik, the former seat of the East German parliament in the old centre Unter den Linden, the former *royal palace* is being re-erected until 2020 and will become the home of the "Humboldt Forum" with museums for non-European cultures and a range of other scientific institutions and libraries as an extension of the Museumsinsel. Potsdamer Platz was Europe's largest building site in the 1990s but has since successfully established itself as a new city centre. Berliners have grown used to the glass central train station located close to the government quarter, which was opened in 2006, and the old west end around the *Gedächtniskirche (memorial church)* has also undergone a splendid redevelopment. The area fell slightly into obscurity when the entire city began to look eastward after the fall of the wall; but since then, certain examples of post-war architecture have been knocked down or – in the case of the historic Zoo Palast cinema or the Bikini Haus shopping centre – extensively refurbished.

The site of a portion of the wall is now the site of the *modern buildings of the government district*. From the dome of the Reichstag you can see to Potsdamer Platz in the south, the monumental glass roof of the main station to the north, the Federal Chancellery to the west and the offices of the MPs to the east. Many politicians and their advisers walk to their parliamentary debates and you will be surprised at how many famous people you will come across in the nearby restaurants and cafés. And, there is something else that is only possible in a city like Berlin: first and foremost, people are thought of as people. Whether somebody is famous or not is purely secondary. *Live and let live* – that's Berlin's motto. Berliners expect to be treated as an individual and are prepared to treat others as such.

In the new seat of power

People of 186 nationalities live in Berlin. Since the financial crisis, the city has become a popular destination for Spaniards and Israelis also enjoy immersing themselves into the *creative Berlin scene* to transform their ideas into reality. At least 200,000 Russians and Poles, together with Ukrainians and Czechs live in Berlin where it can be witnessed first hand how a divided country is growing together and how Europe is becoming more unified as well – after all, Berlin is the only capital city in Europe that is located both in the east and west! Many Russians and Ukrainians who have settled in Berlin are Jewish and this has led to *everyday Jewish culture* once again finding its rightful place in the city. If you stroll around the area near Oranienburger Straße in Mitte, you will come across a Jewish school and cafés and restaurants serving Jewish and oriental specialities. On the other hand, life in the former western inner-city areas, especially Kreuzberg, Neukölln and Wedding, is characterised by the *Turkish way of life*. You can see large Turkish families bartering for crates of aubergines and grapes at the markets or discussing things with friends while traders praise their goods at the top of their voices. Quite an experience! During the coming years, a further layer of diversity will be added by the recent wave of refugees. Nearly 80,000 people claimed asylum in Berlin in 2015, most of them from Syria.

Throughout Berlin's 780-year history newcomers to the city have often brought in-novative *cultural and economic impulses* with them. Be it Huguenots, Bohemians or Silesians, their customs and traditions have left a mark on the city, especially on the culinary sector. *Bouletten* (or *Buletten*) for example is a French word for meatballs that have become a Berlin speciality. In the past, people facing religious persecution in particular were drawn to the Spree as Prussia's regents were known far and wide for their *religious tolerance*. In 1701, during the reign of Friedrich I, a church was built for the Protestant Huguenots – the French Cathedral – and the St.-Hedwigs-Kathedrale was built at the end of the 18th century as a Catholic house of worship for the Silesians. In 1886, Europe's largest synagogue – with seating for 3,200 people – was opened on Oranienburger Straße. This was destroyed in World War II and has only been partially reconstructed.

Over the years, Berlin has played a *central role in world history* on many an occasion. Memories of the Nazi dictatorship, the persecution of the Jews and the terrible con-sequences of World War II are kept alive with countless memorials and remembrance sites. Although the inner city was badly bombed, many historical buildings have been preserved or reconstructed. The Staatsoper Unter den Linden, Berliner Dom, the Schauspielhaus, as well as the German and French Cathedrals on Gendarmenmarkt are magnificent examples of this. And, there is the Museumsinsel with its *unique ensemble of stately Classicist buildings* with archaeological and art collections that are now all open to the public after the completion of lengthy reconstruction work.

Of course, the *recent past* has also left its mark. Many of the young people who live in, or visit, Berlin never experienced the divided city themselves. This makes me-morials such as the Wall Documentation Museum on Bernauer Straße or the Stasi prison Hohenschöbhausen even more important than ever before. The drone of a Douglas DC 3, a transport plane from the time of the airlift in 1948/49, when sup-plies to the western sector of the city had to be masterminded completely from the air as a result of the Soviet blockade, brings back memories of that period whenever it takes off – on special occasions – for flights over Berlin. French, English, Russian and American educational institutions and cultural centres still bear witness to the former presence of the *four Allied occupying powers*. Some Berlin children visit a French music school while others attend a college with a pronounced emphasis on Russian studies. The 400,000 trees that were planted along the streets to make life in the walled-in city more bearable have also remained to this day.

> **This green metropolis adds quality of life**

In fact hardly any other comparable city has *as many parks and green spaces* as Berlin. And the residents of Berlin are similarly "green" when they think about the quality of life in their city. Almost 42 per cent of all their journeys are made on foot or by bike and 27 per cent use public transport. Only half of all households have a car. An increas-ing number of visitors to Berlin can now be seen pedalling hard around the city and there are an enormous number of places where bikes can be rented. Berlin is also

An institution on Berlin's nightlife scene: Clärchens Ballhaus

the secret *organic food capital* with more specialist shops per head than any other German city.

The only problem is the economy. Dealing with the results of 40 years as a divided city is not as easy to come to grips with as many people had hoped. And progress is painfully slow. In the past, the city was kept alive under two opposing political systems and, today, Berlin is still finding it difficult to exist without a stable, efficient economy that has evolved over decades. In spite of the rapidly increasing number of jobs in the service sector, Berlin has to live with a current unemployment rate of 10 per cent. However, the city is making the most of its potential as a *base for scientific institutions*. The universities, colleges, research and scientific organisations are important employers providing around 200,000 jobs. Business in the *creative sector is also booming* – especially in the IT field and design branch. Innovative fashion labels are attracting attention and upcycling is the latest craze, i.e. transforming old materials into new fashion. Today many companies in the capital are focusing on creating a sustainable and ecological business. Time and time again people from Berlin have been successful in establishing themselves as avant-garde businesses and product designers. There are ideas everywhere, but Berlin is where they become reality. And you may well feel the same as many local residents who, despite seeing their city day in, day out, continuously discover exciting new things and are often surprised at how much they didn't know before. *Berlin is like a lucky-dip* – you never know what you're going to come across next!

The perfect place for the adventurous and creative

WHAT'S HOT

1 Multicultural delights

Exotic bites to eat Markthalle Neun (Eisenbahnstr. 9 | www. markthalleneun.de) (photo) in Kreuzberg transforms into a world snack bar on Thursdays from 5pm at its *Street Food Thursday* event: Thai tapioca dumplings, Mexican tacos, German cheese noodle specialities, Peruvian ceviche, Nigerian fufu and Korean buns are all on the menu. Street food trucks also arrive on Sundays (noon–6pm) in the courtyard of the *Kulturbrauerei* in Prenzlauer Berg (www.street foodaufachse.de).

Upcycling

2

Old into new ⊘ The trend of transforming waste into creative items has now spread to fashion in Berlin. Stylish products made from old materials are available at the *Upcycling Fashion Store (Anklamer Str. 17 | Mitte | upcycling-fashion.com) (photo)* and the alteration studio *Bis es mir vom Leibe fällt (Frankenstr. 1 | Schöneberg | www.bisesmirvomleibefaellt.de)* which remodels discarded favourite clothes. Accessories and toys made from waste can also be found at *Upcycling deluxe (Kastanienallee 22 | Prenzlauer Berg | www. upcycling-deluxe.com)*.

3 Ready for takeoff?

Playground for everyone You don't need water to do water sports; sailing or kite surfing can be done on asphalt. Take your board and kite out to the *Tempelhofer Feld* (see p. 60) where you can really hit high speeds *(photo)*. The *Berliner Kiteschule (www.berliner-kiteschule. de)* offers courses. If you prefer to take things easier, book a unicycle session at *Dingadu (dingadu.de)* or rent a pair of skis in winter and take advantage of the prepared cross-country trail *(www.nordisch-aktiv.de)*.

(Electro)mobile in Berlin

Like a rocket 🌐 Travelling around Berlin can involve covering some long distances, and Berliners try to avoid damaging the environment as they make their way around the city. If you like travelling on two wheels then you can take advantage of one of the countless bike rental services *(photo)*. For an overview see *www.berlin.de/tourismus/adressen/fahrrad verleih.* Deutsche Bahn's "Call a Bike" service (see p. 129) also has multiple stations in the city – but if you're looking for an easier option then why not try an e-bike? *E-Bike Tours (Chausseestraße 124 | Mitte | e-bike-touren-berlin.de)* rents these out at 15 euros for three hours (reservation required). It isn't recommended for visitors to travel round Berlin by car, but if you absolutely have to then you can rent one of 350 electric cars from the car-sharing company *Multicity,* with rates starting at 20 cents per minute *(www.multicity-carsharing.de).* 100% of the electricity used by these small Citroën C-Zero cars comes from renewable sources.

Action speaks...

...louder than words The *Haus der guten Taten, Coeco* ("Good Deed House") at the *Potsdamer-Platz-Arkaden (www.coeo-berlin.de)* really lives up to its name. The welfare organisation sells products made in special workshops by handicapped people; the profits flow back into social projects The *Guerrilla-Gardeners (www.facebook.com/guerillagardening) (photo)* come armed with bulbs and rakes. Their aim? To beautify the city and green public spaces for the benefit of all – and, if there is a need, this can even be in a building skip or at the former Tempelhof airport.

IN A NUTSHELL

ALTERNATIVE CULTURE

Off theatres, small hip clubs and concert venues in hidden courtyards: you can discover Berlin's real charm if you venture beyond the highly-subsidised cultural palaces. Only those who have been to a performance in the *Ballhaus Ost* or listened to a punk band in *Schokoladen* (Choc Shop) will know what this means. This is where locals and newcomers have fought for some cultural freedom to make it possible for them to experiment with new kinds of performing arts way off the beaten track. This is where you can get a close-up view of the origins of new movements in music, theatre and art! Berlin's nightlife always has something novel to offer: new clubs are opening all the time in abandoned buildings or old factories. However, these are increasingly located outside the city centre and rented legally. Due to rising rents and advancing regeneration, the scene has been left with fewer and fewer spaces to use; but if you're a member of the right Facebook group then you can still let loose at one of the illegal open-air parties during the summer, which are easy enough to organise with just a sound system and a space in a park.

ART METROPOLIS

With its more than 440 galleries and numerous collections, Berlin is one of the most important art markets in the world, The works of over 6,000 domestic and international artists are displayed, bought and sold here, and big names

Photo: Fashion Week, Showcase Lena Hoschek

Bars on the banks of the Spree, the rebuilding of the royal palace, the charm of East Germany in your hotel room – anything is possible

such as Ai Weiwei and Olafur Eliasson have long had workshops in the city. However, their commercial success is not shared by every artist in Berlin: 95% of them are unable to support themselves with their art and are forced to take on side jobs. Nonetheless, with its rents and living costs still comparatively low, Berlin offers better conditions than cities such as Paris, London or New York. That's what makes the city such a magnet for artists, along with major events such as the *Berlin Art Week* and the *Gallery Weekend Berlin*.

COURTYARD ARCHITECTURE

Berlin is famous for its courtyard ensembles. It is not at all rare to find between two and eight blocks of flats, one behind the other, connected by courtyards and passageways. This style of architecture, typical to Berlin, has regained its former fame partly thanks to the revamped Hackesche Höfe in Mitte. Other examples of skilful courtyard redevelopment in Mitte are the Heckmann-Höfe on Oranienburger Straße, the Sophie-Gips-Höfe on

creative industries, producing everything from furniture and clothes racks to lamps and fashion. They generate over 16.6 billion euros of revenue each year – a growing market that has achieved international recognition. The most important event in the industry is the annual festival *DMY International Design Festival Berlin (www.dmy-berlin.com)* with exhibitions and experimental designs around a focus topic. New blood is provided by the 3,000 students of fashion, product and communication design at the four state colleges and countless private institutions.

FASHION

The trend scouts of the major fashion firms regularly come to Berlin to get inspiration from the imaginative, daring outfits worn by those living in the "in" districts Mitte, Neukölln and Friedrichshain. Fashion is a big issue, not least because of the *Fashion Week* (end of Jan and beginning of July). Some Berlin designers sew one-off garments in backrooms and sell them out front. But the man on the streets does not pay much attention to fashion. Most people in Berlin are more interested in being comfortably dressed. And in some districts you could almost believe that tracksuits (not the fashionablekind, mind you) and flip-flops are considered chic...

Sophienstraße and the Kurt-Berndt-Höfe on Neue Schönhauser Straße. The latter was built for the Metropol Palast Company in 1911/12. After being given back to its former owners, the building was remodelled and modernised in the late 1990s.

DESIGN

Unesco has recognised Berlin as a "City of Design", making it one of more than 100 cities in the global Creative City Network founded by the organisation. This grouping – founded by the United Nations Educational, Scientific and Cultural Organisation – is intended to help cities convert their creative potential into economic development. According to the Economic Senate, around 200,000 Berliners currently work in the so-called

GREEN, GREENEST

Berlin residents really know how to save energy. According to statistics, they produce less CO_2 per inhabitant than anywhere else in Germany! And only every second household – that means every third resident – has a car. Several large companies and state institutions, including the federal buildings and German Bundestag, obtain their heat from power stations fired with vegetable oil and their water is warmed by solar energy. The federal headquarters of the Christian Democratic Party and the new premises of the Green Party's Heinrich Böll Foundation are also equipped with photovoltaic panels. If you are interested, you can take a tour in a solar boat *(tel. 0151 54 22 80 44 | www.solarpolis.de)* to become acquainted with the sights and buildings from the water. Many locals also try to make sure that their groceries are organic and come from the region. Countless large and small organic markets are flourishing although, compared to the average in Germany, the net household income in Berlin is rather modest. *Original Unverpackt* in Kreuzberg (see p. 80) is Germany's first ever packaging-free supermarket, where you need to bring your own containers in order to buy everything from pasta to toothpaste or vodka. The *Veganz* supermarket chain (see p. 79) offers everything any vegan could possibly need, with branches in Prenzlauer Berg, Friedrichshain and Kreuzberg.

LOVE OF ANIMALS

People in Berlin seem to be crazy about anything on four legs. Dogs in particular are real favourites and pedestrians always have to look at least one step ahead to avoid treading on a "stinking landmine". But dog poo is not the only problem; our canine friends simply do not have enough space to run about in. The legal exercise areas in the Volkspark in Friedrichshain and Hasenheide in Kreuzberg are notoriously overcrowded. That not everybody is capable of dealing with this becomes clear if you visit the animal shelter on the northeastern outskirts of the city. Covering an area of 40 acres – including a pet cemetery – it is the largest of its kind in Europe. As many as 12,000 animals are cared for by a staff of around 75 every year. *www.tierschutz-berlin.de*

MAJOR AIRPORT

There is no end to the squabbling over the expansion of Schönefeld Airport

Skies over Berlin – Hackesche Höfe at the Hackescher Markt

to create a new major airport. After morer than 20 years of construction, the opening date is currently set for 2019 – postponement is possible. The people of Berlin are manning the barricades to protest about flight paths. South Berlin will be especially subjected to aircraft noise. Local residents rightly fear not only a decrease in their quality of life but also in the price of their property. What's more, it already looks like the new airport will be too small to handle the many flights into and out of Berlin. As a result, some are now arguing that Tegel should continue to operate even after the opening of BER, in deviation from the original plans.

MULTICULTURAL

People from 186 nations can be found in Berlin. Some streets – particularly in Neukölln, Kreuzberg, Moabit and Wedding – are dominated by Arab and Turkish culture. But, life in the city would not be the same without the supermarkets, bakeries, cafés and restaurants of the Russians (mainly in Charlottenburg and Marzahn), Poles and the workers

FOR FILM BUFFS

Good Bye Lenin! – Wolfgang Becker's prize-winning tragicomedy (2003) about life in East Berlin at the time of reunification

Victoria – This 2015 film follows the title character – a young Spanish woman – on a night out clubbing in Berlin that ends in a bank robbery. Director Sebastian Schipper filmed the entire movie in a single take, so the final product is completely unedited

formerly contracted to help out in East Germany – the Vietnamese. Unemployment is especially high among migrants. Many Turks who came to Berlin as immigrant workers almost 50 years ago found themselves out of work after the Reunification of Germany as factories and firms closed down one after the other. There are hardly any jobs for unskilled workers without a school leaving qualification and it is disastrous that 15 per cent of the young people from migrant families living in Berlin are unable to start an apprenticeship because they lack this basic qualification. The Berlin Senate is attempting to solve this problem through new education campaigns such as making it compulsory to attend a day-care centre with special language training before starting school.

ON THE WATERFRONT

Hardly any other city in Europe is blessed with as many lakes, rivers and canals as Berlin. There are more than 500 km (310 miles) of shoreline where you can go for a walk, sunbathe and even live! Most of the restaurants and clubs with a view of the water are located near the Oberbaumbrücke in Kreuzberg and Friedrichshain. Beach bars with deck chairs on the shores of the Spree and, of course, a vast number of places where you can swim in summer – all boasting a water quality standard from good to excellent – invite you take a break. A highlight is the more than 100 year old ● *Strandbad Wannsee (April–Oct daily 10am–6pm, in summer until 8/9pm | admission 5.50 euros | www.berlinerbaeder. de/baeder/strandbad-wannsee | S 1, 7 Nikolassee)*, Europe's biggest lake swimming bath. Guests get the feeling of being at the Baltic Sea with its fine sand and wicker beach chairs with a hood.

For Berliners with green fingers: urban gardening in the Prinzessinnengärten

RISEN FROM THE RUINS

Destroyed in World War II, the ruins then blown up as ordered by East Berlin authorities, now shortly before the resurrection: After the Palast der Republik, the former cultural centre of the GDR, was torn down, now the palace facades are being erected on the Schlossinsel between Spree and Spree canal. Behind them, the *Humboldt-Forum* containing Berlin's ethnological collections and several science institutions will find their place.

SCIENCE

Did you know that Berlin is one of the leading cities for science in Europe? Around 200,000 scientists, students and other specialists teach, study and carry out research in four universities, four polytechnics, the Charité Medical University, four art academies, more than 30 private universities and 70 research institutes. Every year in June, they join up forces and organise an evening of events that gives an interesting insight into the achievements of individual institutes and research centres. *www.langenachtderwissenschaften.de*

URBAN GARDENING

Spinach and leek can be seen growing in the city and remind inhabitants of how vegetables are actually grown. A lot of Berlin's wasteland has been transformed into vegetable plots such as the Prinzessinnengärten *(prinzessinnengarten.net)* at the Moritzplatz in Kreuzberg. The gardens also have their own café which uses the freshly picked vegetables in their delicious soups and bakes in summer. On the Neukölln side of the city's former airport, Tempelhofer Feld, you'll also see pumpkins and courgettes growing in abundance. Corn and red cabbage are also grown and harvested even on main city thoroughfares such as Torstraße in the Mitte district. In this way at certain times in late summer, Berliners can live from hand to mouth.

SIGHTSEEING

CITY **WHERE TO START?**
Alexanderplatz (141 F2–3)
(m L3–4) with the TV tower is the ideal place to start your visit. It is easy to reach by underground (U 2, 5, 8) or on the district line (S 3, 5, 7, 75). The entrance to the public car park for 650 vehicles is off the central strip of the Alexanderplatz 6 street. The Rotes Rathaus, the seat of the Lord Mayor of Berlin, is also right on "Alex" and it's just a short walk to reach the Museumsinsel with the Cathedral, the Pergamon and Bode Museums and many other institutions.

Even Berliners sometimes have difficulties recognising certain parts of their city. Those who haven't been into the city centre for several months will find new buildings have popped up on what were empty pieces of land, new bridges have appeared where there was no crossing before, and newly-opened museums waiting for them to explore. No other European city is changing so quickly!

The construction boom has also taken hold of the western sector of the city; new hotels are springing up everywhere, rundown buildings on Kurfürstendamm – such as the famous Kranzlereck – have simply been demolished and modern structures have taken their place. The airy buildings in the government district never fail to captivate viewers and visitors have to queue up to

И МНЕ ВЫЖИТЬ

МЕРТНОЙ ЛЮБВИ

Berlin is changing at a breathtaking pace. New museums, whole streets and buildings make the city like a fascinating kaleidoscope

see inside the Reichstag with its glass dome. There is still plenty of scope for inspired architecture and new ideas, for example at the Ostbahnhof where a new commercial district has been built. And then there is the reconstruction of Berlin's former royal palace. A new residential and office district for many thousand people, the so-called Europacity, is being built north of the main station that was opened in 2006. The inner city is gradually starting to show itself at its best and anybody who walks through the restored Brandenburger Tor today will find it difficult to believe how desolate Pariser Platz behind it was for so many years. Many visitors see a city that didn't exist in this form several years ago. It may be obvious that the shiny new glass and concrete monoliths on Potsdamer Platz must have been built relatively recently, but planners in the Nikolaiviertel and on Unter den Linden have instead chosen to imitate architectural styles from centuries gone by. However, these reconstructions have attracted ridicule just as

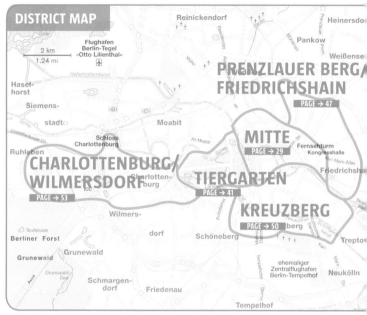

DISTRICT MAP

Reinickendorf

Heinersdo

Pankow

Flughafen
Berlin-Tegel
»Otto Lilienthal«

2 km
1.24 mi

Weißense

Hasel-
horst

Hohenzollernkanal

Siemens-

PRENZLAUER BERG/
FRIEDRICHSHAIN

PAGE → 47

stadt

Moabit

Schloss
Charlottenburg

Alt-Moabit

MITTE

PAGE → 29

Fernsehturm
Kongresshalle

Ruhleben

Charlottenburger Ch.

Alt-Marx-Allee

CHARLOTTENBURG/
WILMERSDORF

Charlotten-
burg

TIERGARTEN

PAGE → 41

Friedrichsha

PAGE → 53

ICC

Wilmers-

KREUZBERG

PAGE → 50

berg

Treptov

Teufelssee

dorf

Schöneberg

Berliner Forst

Grunewald

Grunewald

Grunewald-
See

ehemaliger
Zentralflughafen
Berlin-Tempelhof

Neukölln

Schmargen-
dorf

Friedenau

Tempelhof

The map shows the location of the most interesting districts. There is a detailed map of each district on which each of the sights described is numbered.

much as the city's lack of skyscrapers. The residents of Berlin prefer to keep things within reasonable limits and there is still not enough economic power to warrant a business district like the one in Frankfurt am Main.

On the other hand, culture ranks very highly in Berlin. With over 200 museums, collections and archives, Berlin has a superlative museum landscape. Painting, everyday culture, technical and local history – there is such a great variety that it would take months even to get some sort of general overview. And, on top of that, there is always something new.

The courage to take cultural risks has a long tradition in Berlin. Does any other city have a museum specially built for an excavated altar? It is not without reason

that the *Pergamon Museum,* opened in 1930, is one of the most popular in the city and attracts around 1 million visitors annually (but there is only restricted access until 2019 due to refurbishments). And that can be said about the entire *Museumsinsel,* too. The ensemble of five museums houses artistic treasures that can only be matched worldwide by the Louvre in Paris and the Hermitage in Saint Petersburg. It was Crown Prince Friedrich Wilhelm came up with the idea of a centre for art and history. The *Old Museum* (Engraving Collection), the *New Museum*, *Bode-Museum* and *National Gallery* (19th century painting and sculpture) and *Pergamon Museum* (Collection of Antiquities, Middle-Eastern Museum, Museum for Islamic Art, from 2019 ancient Egyptian architecture) developed between 1825 and 1930. The *New Museum* has been remodelled to plans by the British architect David Chipperfield and, since autumn 2009, is home to the collection of the Egyptian Museum including the famous bust of Queen Nefertiti. The *Bode-Museum,* with its impressive dome, presents exhibits from the *Museum for Byzantine Art,* parts of the *coin collection* and sculptures. Since 1957, the *Stiftung Preußischer Kulturbesitz* (Prussian Cultural Property Foundation) has been in charge of the *Berlin State Museums, State Library, Secret State Archives* and the *Ibero-American Institute,* as well as the *Institute for Music Research* with its *Musikinstrumenten-Museum.* The latter has its home in the Culture Forum in Tiergarten, the West Berlin counterpart to the Museumsinsel. Entrance fees to the Berlin State Museums range from 8 to 12

euros but higher prices are charged for special exhibitions. Information on all museums, guided tours and special exhibitions: *tel. 030 24 74 98 88* or *www.mu seumsportal-berlin.de.*

MITTE

The treasures on Museumsinsel are considered highlights from the history of art by experts around the world, the Television Tower with its 203 m (666 ft) high viewing platform is a real crowd-puller on sunny days, and taking a photo of the city's most important landmark – the Brandenburger Tor – is a must. *Mitte* has, by far, more sights than any other district of Berlin. Take a walk along Unter den Linden and you will discover the historical heart of the city. The *Humboldt-Universität*, for example, where

★ **Fernsehturm**
Best view of the city in the former centre of Berlin → p. 34

★ **Gendarmenmarkt**
The city's most beautiful square with buildings from the 18th and 19th centuries → p. 36

★ **Museuminsel**
Impressive ensemble consisting of five huge museums → p. 38

★ **Unter den Linden**
Wilhelmian Boulevard with magnificent historical buildings → p. 40

★ **Brandenburger Tor**
Berlin's symbol on Pariser Platz now shines in all its glory → p. 41

★ **Potsdamer Platz**
The new, urban centre in the former border area → p. 45

★ **Tempelhofer Feld**
A former airfield open to everyone as an urban playground → p. 60

★ **Reichstag**
A successful mix of old and new along with a wonderful view from the top of the glass dome → p. 46

★ **Jüdisches Museum Berlin**
A gripping exhibition of Jewish culture in the "lightning bolt" building designed by star architect Daniel Libeskind → p. 52

★ **Schloss Charlottenburg**
Baroque architecture with a magnificent park → p. 55

★ **Schloss Sanssouci**
Potsdam's Prussian jewel – a total work of art with palaces, pavilions and landscaped gardens → p. 62

MARCO POLO HIGHLIGHTS

Hold on tight – the Berliner Dom as seen from a cruise ship

famous scientists such as Albert Einstein and Rudolf Virchow taught. Or the *Zeughaus* with the German Historical Museum. There is also plenty of action in the evening between Gendarmenmarkt, the Nikolai District and Neue Synagoge: the restaurants, bars and clubs will make sure that you'll enjoy yourself until the early hours. The best place to go shopping is around the *Hackescher Markt*. That is where Berlin designers have set up their studios and shops. Modern art is mainly sold north of the Neue Synagoge; the density of international galleries is quite impressive.

◼◼ BERLINER DOM (141 E3) (*ฒ K–L4*)

The cathedral, constructed between 1894 and 1905 under the supervision of the architect Julius Carl Raschdorf, was severely damaged in World War II. The main section of the building only became available for services in the mid-1990s after extensive reconstruction work had been

completed. The altar with the Apostle Wall, the baptismal font and two candelabras are still from the old cathedral. The Hohenzollern crypt is the resting place for around 90 monarchs and members of the Prussian nobility. There is a **INSIDERTIP** wonderful view of the Museumsinsel and the newly built palace from the ⊿ dome! *April–Oct daily 9am–8pm, Nov–March 9am–7pm (no visits during services) | admission 7 euros (three children up to 18 years free) | prayers Mon–Sat noon, Mon–Fri 6pm, services Sun 10am, 6pm, Thu in German and English | several guided tours daily | Am Lustgarten | www.berliner-dom.de | S 3, 5, 7, 75 Hackescher Markt, bus 100 Schlossplatz*

◼◼ **INSIDERTIP** COMPUTERSPIELE-MUSEUM (153 F2) (*ฒ N4*)

An oversized Atari joystick, the first 3-D glasses and lots of game consoles can be tried. 300 exhibits spread over an area of 600 m² (0.15 acres) document the 40 year history of the digital game culture from Pong to Zelda. *Daily 10am–8pm | admission 8 euros | Karl-Marx-Allee 93a | www.computerspielemuseum.de | U 5 Weberwiese*

▣ DDR-MUSEUM (141 E3) *(𝄞 L4)*

Queues and a restricted range of food, tacky jeans, nudist holidays, Erika type-writers and music by Karat and City that can be heard once again over head-phones. The history of life in the GDR over more than 800 m²/8,611 sq ft. *Daily 10am–8pm, Sat until 10pm | admission 7 euros, online from 4 euros | Karl-Liebknecht-Str. 1 | Spreepromenade | www.ddr-museum.de | S 3, 5, 7, 75 Hackescher Markt*

▣ INSIDER TIP▶ DENKMAL DER BÜCHERVERBRENNUNG (141 D4) *(𝄞 K4)*

This memorial on Bebelplatz near the Staatsoper created by the Israeli artist Micha Ullmans commemorates the Burning of the Books on 10 May 1933. Works by Erich Kästner, Bertolt Brecht, Kurt Tucholsky and other authors who the Nazis did not approve of were flung onto the fire. The memorial in a former tram tunnel is conceived as a cleared out li-brary with room for 20,000 books. You look into the empty bookcases through a sheet of glass in the ground. *Bebelplatz | bus 100 Staatsoper*

▣ DEUTSCHES HISTORISCHES MUSEUM (141 D3) *(𝄞 K4)*

The core of the permanent exhibition that was reopened in the Zeughaus in 2006 is formed by the so-called "epoch rooms". The visitors wander through them from the beginnings of German history to the present. Temporary exhibi-tions are shown in the new building designed by Ieoh Ming Pei. *Daily 10am–6pm | admission 8 euros (children under 18 free) | Zeughaus (old building) | Unter den Linden 2 | www.dhm.de | S 3, 5, 7 Hackescher Markt*

▣ DOROTHEENSTADT CEMETERY (140 B1) *(𝄞 J–K3)*

Many of the greats from the world of art and culture have found their final resting place here. Among them are the former Federal President Johannes Rau, Heinrich Mann, Bertolt Brecht, Helene Weigel, Anna Seghers, Heiner Müller, Karl Friedrich Schinkel, Johann Gottlieb Fichte and Georg Wilhelm Friedrich Hegel. The remains of the French cemetery that was set up for the Huguenots in 1780 can also be found within the walls. The old trees

LOW BUDGET

The ● *Gaslaternenmuseum* or Gas Lamp Museum **(150 B3)** *(𝄞 G4) (al-ways open | S 5, 7, 75 Tiergarten)* on the edge of the Tiergarten holds a charming open-air collection of his-toric gas lamps from across Europe, and is free of charge. Visit at sun-set for a particularly atmospheric ex-perience.

You will have a trip past many of the sights in Berlin for the price of a bus ticket by simply taking bus no. 100 from Bahnhof Zoo to Alexanderplatz. Stops at the Siegessäule, Schloss Bellevue, Reichstag and Branden-burger Tor.

The ⚇ *Siegessäule* or Victory Col-umn (see p. 47) **(150 C3)** *(𝄞 G4)* on the Großer Stern square in the Tier-garten offers fantastic views over the entire city, and it costs just 3 euros to climb to the top.

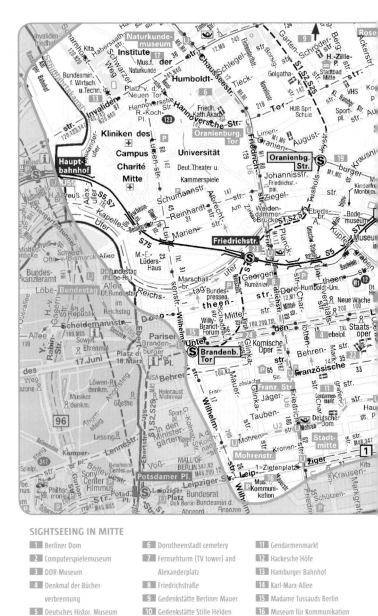

SIGHTSEEING IN MITTE

1 Berliner Dom
2 Computerspielemuseum
3 DDR-Museum
4 Denkmal der Bücher-
  verbrennung
5 Deutsches Histor. Museum
6 Dorotheenstadt cemetery
7 Fernsehturm (TV tower) and
  Alexanderplatz
8 Friedrichstraße
9 Gedenkstätte Berliner Mauer
10 Gedenkstätte Stille Helden
11 Gendarmenmarkt
12 Hackesche Höfe
13 Hamburger Bahnhof
14 Karl-Marx-Allee
15 Madame Tussauds Berlin
16 Museum für Kommunikation

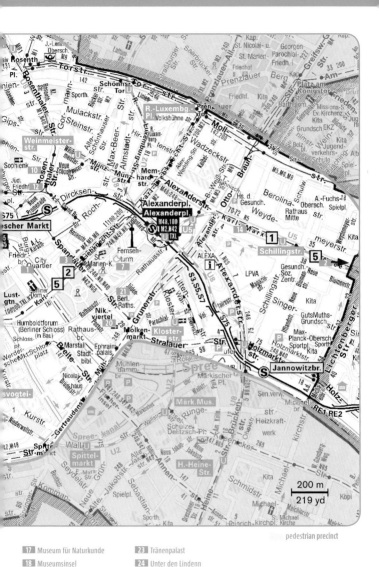

pedestrian precinct

World-time clock at the base of the Fernsehturm on Alexanderplatz

make this a quiet spot to escape from the mad rush of the city and catch your breath. *Chausseestr. 126 | U 6 Naturkundemuseum*

7 FERNSEHTURM AND ALEXANDERPLATZ ☆
(141 F2–3) (*L3–4*)

The ★ ● *Fernsehturm* is the second highest television tower in Europe and one of the city's landmarks. Built between 1966 and 1969, the tower with its glass sphere and overall height of 365 m (1,197 ft) can be seen from almost everywhere in the centre of the city. It is hard to find a place on the platform 203 m (666 ft) above the ground on cloudless days. A text message service makes it possible for you to not have to queue or wait: visitors are sent a text when it is their turn. Then the express lift will catapult you up to the platform in a mere 40 seconds. The restaurant *Sphere* *(tel. 030 24 75 75 87 5 | Moderate)* above the viewing platform revolves around its own axis twice an hour. If it is a clear day, you will be able to see a good 40 km (25 miles). *Nov–Feb daily 10am–midnight, March–Oct 9am–midnight | admission 13 euros, VIP ticket 19.50 euros (no waiting time!) | Panoramastr. 1a | www.tv-turm.de* *Alexanderplatz* at the base of the television tower (on the other side of the railway tracks) was named in honour of Tsar Alexander I in 1805 and formerly used as a parade ground and market. Today, it is overrun with people on a shopping spree and visitors to the television tower. The square completely changed its appearance after it was restored, the *Kaufhof* department store renovated, and *C & A* moved into the listed *Berolinahaus* completed in 1929. Only the *World-time Clock* and *Friendship between Nations Fountain* bring back memories of life in former East Berlin. The huge building site in front of the Rotes Rathaus relates to the construction of a new U-Bahn line from Alexanderplatz to the Brandenburg Gate, which is scheduled to open in 2020 – at the same time as the Humboldt Forum in the Berlin Palace. At that point, there are also plans to move the *Neptunbrunnen* fountain back to its former location in front of the castle. The god of the sea and his trident have been in exile in front of the offices of the mayor of Berlin since 1969. *Alexanderplatz | U/S Alexanderplatz | bus 100 Spandauer Straße*

■8■ FRIEDRICHSTRASSE
(140 C1–6) (*ɸ K3–6*)

Friedrichstraße was already the place to go for some fun in the 1920s. The street, some 3.5 km (2 miles) long, that crosses the Mitte district from north to south was lined with theatres, cabarets and bars. Before the Reunification, the Berlin Wall cut the street in two and the border crossing here was the famous Checkpoint Charlie. Today, there are only a few sandbags piled up high and a control booth to remind you of this. Stylish business premises, such as the *Quartier 206* with its exclusive boutiques, now dominate the skyline. The *Galeries Lafayette*, with

its glass atrium, is another architectural highlight. The *Friedrichstadt-Palast* was already famous for its revues when this area was still part of East Germany. *U/S Friedrichstraße*

■9■ GEDENKSTÄTTE BERLINER MAUER
(146 B5) (*ɸ K2*)

A section of the original wall has been left standing. On the open-air site, listening stations offer information about tragic escape efforts and the former line of the border. The documentation centre shows an exhibition (newly devised in 2014) on everyday life on Bernauer Straße in the walled city that is no longer in Mitte but already part of the district of Wedding. *Tue–Sun 10am–6pm | admission free | Bernauer Str. 111| www.berliner-mauer-gedenkstaette.de | S1, 2, 25 Nordbahnhof*

■10■ INSIDER TIP ► GEDENKSTÄTTE STILLE HELDEN (141 E2) (*ɸ L3*)

This impressive archive uses multimedia technology to present the biographies of Jews and those who protected them in the Third Reich. *Daily 10am–8 pm | admission free | Rosenthaler Str. 39 | www.gedenkstaette-stille-helden.de | S3, 5, 7, 75 Hackescher Markt*

BERLIN ON THE WATER

The most pleasant way to discover the historic Mitte or government districts is by taking a cruise. Numerous ships chug up and down the Spree all year long. The stops include the Museumsinsel, Friedrichstraße and the Haus der Kulturen der Welt. A round trip from Mitte via Kreuzberg to Charlottenburg and back to Mitte along the Spree and Landwehr Canal is particularly interesting. On this three-hour tour you will not only see most of the main sights in the city, the onboard "cityscape guide" (most of the time the captain himself) will also give you lots of information about everyday life and customs of the people of Berlin. *Information on sailing times and prices: tel. 030 5 36 36 00 | www.sternundkreis.de.*

Karl-Marx-Allee – the city's former monumental socialist boulevard

⑪ GENDARMENMARKT ★
(141 D4–5) *(⊠ K4)*

With its buildings from the 18th and 19th centuries this is considered the most beautiful square in the city. The *Schauspielhaus*, which was built by Karl Friedrich Schinkel between 1818 and 1821 and now serves as a concert hall, and the Schiller Monument are framed by the Französische and Deutsche Dom. The *French Cathedral (tower April–Oct daily 10am–7 pm, Nov–March daily 10:30am–6:30pm, organ recital Tue–Fri 12:30pm, Huguenot Musem Tue–Sun noon–5pm | admission tower 3 euros, Huguenot Museum 2 euros | Gendarmenmarkt 5)* suffered severe damage during the war and was reconstructed in 1983. It was built between 1701 and 1705 for the 8,000 Huguenots living in the city. An exhibition in the cathedral provides information on the life of these Calvinist Protestants. The 70 m (230 ft) high ⚡tower was built from 1780–85 and you have a magnificent view over the historical heart of Berlin from the top. The *German Cathedral* at the opposite side of the square is no longer used as a church today but as an exhibition space on German democratic history. *www. gendarmenmarkt.de | U 6 Stadtmitte*

⑫ HACKESCHE HÖFE (141 E2) *(⊠ L3)*

The Hackesche Höfe were built between 1905 and 1907 and this labyrinth of interconnecting courtyards has since become an architectural highlight. Restaurants, a cinema, galleries, a cabaret and boutiques have been set up in them. Many Jews used to live in the area with its long tradition as a centre of craft and retail businesses. The partially restored *New Synagogue* (see p. 38) on Oranienburger Straße bears witness to this past. *S 3, 5, 7, 75 Hackescher Markt*

⑬ HAMBURGER BAHNHOF
(151 E1) *(⊠ J3)*

The former railway station has been transformed into a museum with a total area

wide. Only rubble was left of what was once Frankfurter Straße after the war. The symbol of this impressive avenue, with its housing blocks that are nearly 300 m (984 ft) long and up to 9 storeys high, are the two towers at Frankfurter Tor that were modelled on the towers of the cathedrals on Gendarmenmarkt. The buildings were mainly built using the rubble of bombed houses. On 17 June 1953, the worker's revolt that was brutally crushed flared up on this street which was called "Stalinallee" until 1961. *U 5 Frankfurter Tor*

15 MADAME TUSSAUDS BERLIN

(140 B4) (*∅ J4*)

The famous waxworks museum near Brandenburger Tor has life-sized models ranging from Berlin's former Lord Mayor Klaus Wowereit to Johnny Depp, Madonna and The Beatles, football stars and Angela Merkel. *Daily 10am–7pm (Aug until 7:30pm) | admission 23.50 euros, online from 14 euros (tickets are up to 5 euros cheaper from the BVG ticket machines!) | Unter den Linden 74 | www.madametus sauds.com | U/S Brandenburger Tor*

16 INSIDER TIP MUSEUM FÜR KOMMUNIKATION (140 C6) (*∅ K5*)

The Museum for Communication is considered the oldest postal museum in the world. The visitor is presented with a fascinating exhibition including a computer gallery, interactive exhibits, robots, Philip Reis' first telephone apparatus and the most famous stamps ever: the red and the blue Mauritius. *Tue 9am–8pm, Wed–Fri 9am–5pm, Sat/Sun 10am–6pm | admission 4 euros | Leipziger Str. 16 | www.mfk-berlin.de | U 2, 6 Stadtmitte*

17 MUSEUM FÜR NATURKUNDE

(140 A1) (*∅ J3*

This collection with more than 25 million zoological, paleontological, mineralogi-

---

of 140,000 square feet where especially art from the past 60 years is on display; most of it was provided by the collector Erich Marx. The core of the collection is formed by works by Robert Rauschenberg, Roy Lichtenstein, Andy Warhol, Cy Twombly, Anselm Kiefer and Joseph Beuys and added to this an excellent permanent loan from the Flick Collection is shown in special exhibitions. *Tue–Fri 10am–6pm (Thu until 8pm), Sat/Sun 11am–6pm | admission 8 euros, with special exhibitions 14 euros | Invalidenstr. 50/51 | www.hamburgerbahn hof.de | S/UHauptbahnhof*

14 INSIDER TIP KARL-MARX-ALLEE

(153 E–F2) (*∅ M–O 3–4*)

Not only the architecture of this boulevard, the longest listed ensemble of its kind in Germany, points towards Moscow. Socialist realism, also called the "Stalinist gingerbread style", can be seen on both sides of this impressive road built between 1952 and 1960 that is nearly 90 m (295 ft)

cal and geological objects is world class. Since 2015, the museum has been the proud home of **INSIDER TIP** "Tristan Otto" – one of the best-preserved Tyrannosaurus rex skeletons anywhere in the world. 170 of its approximately 300 bones are original. Hundreds of specimens provide an overview of our indigenous fauna. *Tue–Fri 9:30am–6pm, Sat/Sun 10am–6pm | admission 8 euros | Invalidenstr. 43 | www.naturkundemuseum-berlin.de | U 6 Naturkundemuseum*

18 MUSEUMSINSEL ★ ●
(141 D–E 2–3) (ℳ K–L 3–4)
All museums *daily 10am–6pm, Thu until 8pm, Alte Nationalgalerie, Altes Museum, Bode-Museum closed Mon | www.smb.museum | S 3, 5, 7, 75 Hackescher Markt* Etruscan, Greek and Roman art and sculpture is shown in the *Old Museum*. Stone sculptures and figures made of clay and bronze, friezes, vases, gold jewellery and precious silver will make you fully aware of the magnificence of this culture.

The restored *Bode-Museum*, with its splendid collection of sculptures, the Museum for Byzantine Art (with pictures from the early medieval period until the late 18th century) and collection of 500,000 rare coins, is the pride and joy of Berlin.

After extensive restoration, the *National Gallery*, with its valuable paintings and sculptures from the 19th century, is now one of the most beautiful museum buildings in Berlin. Works by artists such as Menzel, Schadow and Blechen tell us a lot about the architecture, fashion and spirit of the Imperial period.

The *Pergamon Museum* was built between 1910 and 1930 specifically to house the Pergamon Altar that the engineer Carl Humann had discovered in Turkey in the 19th century and spent 20 years restoring. The sculptural frieze, 113 m (370 ft) long, is one of the great masterpieces of Hellenist art and shows the battle of the gods against the giants (closed until 2019 for restoration work). The majestic market gate from Milet (130 AD), a showpiece of Roman architecture, can be seen in an adjacent hall. The collections of Islamic and Near-Eastern art are also unique in the world. The tiled Processional Way of Babylon with its ornate depictions of lions is simply outstanding.

Since 2009, the world-famous, more than 3,000-year-old, bust of Nefertiti has been on display in the *Neue Museum* along with the Egyptian collection of the Prussian Cultural Property Foundation. The museum, which is one of the city's loveliest, was reconstructed and combined with modern elements to plans drawn up by David Chipperfield. The museum, built by Friedrich August Stüler between 1843 and 1855, was severely damaged in World War II and remained empty for 60 years. The partially restored wall paintings inside are another highlight.

19 NEUE SYNAGOGE *(141 D2) (ℳ K3)*
When it was consecrated in 1866, this was the largest synagogue in the world with seating for 3,200 people. Today, the building on Oranienburger Straße is only used as a memorial site, for exhibitions and as a place of prayer. Once you have passed through security, you will find yourself in front of a glass wall which gives you a view of the former place of worship – today, this is a gravelled, open space. The synagogue was only saved from being burned to the ground on 9 November 1938 by the courageous intervention of a Berlin policeman. In 1943, a bombing raid almost completely destroyed it. The façade and golden dome, with a staircase leading up to it, were renovated since 1988. *April–Sept Mon–Fri 10am–6pm, Sun 10am–7pm, Oct–March Sun–Thu 10am–6pm, Fri 10am–3pm | admission 5 euros, dome 3 euros |*

Oranienburger Str. 28–30 | www.cjuda icum.de | S 1, 2, 25 Oranienburger Straße

🔟 NIKOLAI DISTRICT
(141 E–F 3–4) (📖 L4)

The *Nikolaiviertel* with the Nikolai Church to the south-east of Alexanderplatz is considered the birthplace of the city; this is where the first houses were built in the 13th century. At first glance, it appears that the buildings were constructed in the 18th and 19th centuries but most of them were actually built in the 1980s for Berlin's 750th anniversary as a "best-of collection". *U 2 Klosterstraße*

🔢 ROTES RATHAUS (141 F3) (📖 L4)

You can see the red-brick building that was built between 1861 and 1870 on Alexanderplatz from afar. The main building is in the style of the Italian Renaissance while the bell tower is modelled on Laon Cathedral in France. 36 panels depicting the history of Berlin can be seen on the first floor. The town hall suffered severe damage in World War II and became the seat of the East Berlin Council in 1958, the Senate of West Berlin taking up office in Schöneberg Town Hall. Since the Reunification of Germany, the Red Town Hall has once again become the seat for all Berlin. *Rathausstr. 15 | tel. 030 902 624 11 | www.berlin.de | U/S Alexanderplatz*

🔢 ST.-HEDWIGS-KATHEDRALE
(141 D4) (📖 K4)

At the beginning of the 18th century there were only 700 Catholics in Berlin. This increased to around 10,000 just 30 years later. They had fled to liberal Berlin in the wake of the Silesian Wars and, for that reason, the foundation stone for a new

Magnificent setting for a large collection: Egyptian section in the Neues Museum

church, designed by the architect Jean Legeay together with the royal building director Johann Boumann the Elder, was laid in 1747. It was not until 1773 – almost 30 years after building had started – that the Baroque church could be used. It is modelled on the Pantheon in Rome. It suffered severe bomb damage in World War II but was reconstructed relatively quickly (1952 to 1963). *Mon–Sat 10am–5pm, Sun 1pm–5pm | free admission | Bebelplatz 3 | www.hedwigs-kathedrale.de | U 2 Hausvogteiplatz | bus 100 Staatsoper*

23 TRÄNENPALAST (152 A2) (*Ø K4*)

This hall located in front of the Friedrich-straße S-Bahn station owes its name – "Palace of Tears" – to the many tears that were shed here by those left behind at the former border checkpoint. Today, there is an exhibition that looks at the harassment inflicted by the GDR on everybody who was permitted to cross the border. *Tue–Fri 9am–7pm, Sat/ Sun 10am–6pm | free admission | Reichs-tag-ufer 17 | www.hdg.de/berlin/traenen palast | U/S Friedrichstraße*

24 UNTER DEN LINDEN ★

(140–141 B–D 3–4) (*Ø J–K4*)

The boulevard, which begins at *Branden-burger Tor* and ends at *Berliner Dom*, has still not lost any of its importance as Berlin's intellectual and artistic centre – this is not least due to the Museumsinsel. Starting in the 18th century, this was the site of the *Kronprinzenpalais*, the *Zeug-haus*, as well as the *Staatsoper* and to-day's *Humboldt-Universität*. At the end of the 19th century, the *Berliner Dom* was constructed in the Wilhelmine style. The boulevard was completely devastated during World War II. With the exception of the royal City Palace whose remains the East Berlin city council had blown up in 1950, all other buildings have been restored or replaced. The palace on the banks of the Spree was replaced by the

Form and function in harmony: Bauhaus-Archiv in the Tiergarten

Palast der Republik; during the East German era this was an important cultural centre. It has now been demolished and the former royal palace is being reconstructed on its original site. The information centre *Humboldtbox* provides information on the building site and shows a INSIDER**TIP** model of the city centre. *U/S Brandenburger Tor*

TIERGARTEN

Joggers' favourite park, parliament buildings and shopping – hardly any other district is as varied as Tiergarten.
You have the best panoramic view of the city from the dome of the Reichstag building from where you can see the tented roof of the Sony Center on Potsdamer Platz and the Quadriga, the chariot that crowns Brandenburger Tor. To the west, the golden goddess Victoria on Victory Column beckons over the treetops. Berlin's "green lung", the park which gives this district its name, not only offers the city's residents recreation but also cultural highlights such as the Philharmonie and ● INSIDER**TIP** free concerts in summer in the *English Garden* or Indian pop bands in the House of Cultures of the World.

■ BAUHAUS-ARCHIV (151 D5) (*ØJ H5*)
Fascinating collection on the history of the Bauhaus: furniture, works of art, design by Ludwig Mies van der Rohe, Walter Gropius and others. Gropius designed the museum itself in 1964. *Wed–Mon 10am–5pm | admission Sat–Mon 8, Wed–Fri 7 euros | Klingelhöfer Str. 14 | www.bauhaus. de | bus 100 Lützowplatz*

■ EMBASSY DISTRICT
(150–151 C–D 4–5) (*ØJ G–H5*)
Many embassies have been re-established to the south of the Tiergarten. Diplomats resided here before World War II but only the renovated Japanese and Italian embassies still keep up the tradition from that time. The new embassies of Sweden, Norway, Iceland, Denmark and Finland are architectural highlights in their own right. They share a building complex, the *Embassies of the Nordic Countries (Community House Mon–Fri 10am–7pm, Sat/Sun 11am–4pm | Rauchstr. 1 | tel. 030 5 05 00 | www.nordicembassies.org)*. They organise regular exhibitions, concerts and readings, for like many embassies they consider a cultural programme that is available to the general public as being particularly important. The *Mexican Embassy (Mon–Fri 9am–6pm | Klingelhöferstr. 3 | tel. 030 2 69 32 30 | embamex.sre.gob.mx/alemania)* next door is an avant-garde building with a 18 m (60 ft) high foyer and a spectacular façade. *Bus 100 Nordische Botschaften*

■ BRANDENBURGER TOR ★ ●
(140 A–B4) (*ØJ J4*)
Originally built at the edge of the city as part of the customs wall, today the Brandenburg Gate is the symbol of Berlin. The 20 m (66 ft) high monument has adorned Pariser Platz since 1791; it was built to plans by the architect Carl Gotthard Langhans. The Goddess of Victory, driving her four horses onwards, is regarded as the harbinger of peace, which is why the building was initially named Friedenstor. After his successful campaign, Napoleon humiliated Berlin in 1806 by taking the Quadriga back to Paris. It was not until eight years later, after the War of Liberation, that it was returned to its original location. Victoria was decorated with an Iron Cross, laurel wreath and Prussian eagle in memory of the battle against Napoleon.
Brandenburger Tor was severely damaged during World War II and the city

administrations of East and West Berlin used old plaster models to create a copy of the Quadriga. However, the East German government insisted that the Iron Cross and Prussian eagle be re-

memorial as a picnic spot, as some visitors do. This is frowned upon. An exhibition in the subterranean "Place of Information" provides some context to the Nazi politics of terror. *Information*

The four horses on Brandenburger Tor pulling the Goddess of Victory's chariot

moved and a staff with a wreath of oak leaves placed in the Goddess of Victory's hand. Only after the Reunification of Germany could the old symbols be reinstated. *Pariser Platz | U/S Brandenburger Tor*

◢ DENKMAL FÜR DIE ERMORDETEN JUDEN EUROPAS
(140 A–B 4–5) (*𝄞 J4*)

Built in 2005, this site is Germany's memorial to the more than 6 million Jewish victims of the Holocaust. You may well feel isolated and abandoned as you wander among the 2,700 columns, but that is entirely in line with the intentions of New York architect Peter Eisenman – far more so than if you choose to use the

centre: April–Sept Tue–Sun 10am–8pm, Oct–March 10am–7pm | free admission | Cora-Berliner-Str. 1 | www.stiftung-denk mal.de | U/S Brandenburger Tor

◢ GEDENKSTÄTTE DEUTSCHER WIDERSTAND (151 E4) (*𝄞 H5*)

The courtyard of the former army administration building is where the conspirators behind the attempt on Hitler's life were executed during the night of 20 July 1944. Today, an exhibition gives an insight into how people struggled against the Nazi dictatorship. *Mon–Wed, Fri 9am–6pm, Thu 9am–8pm, Sat/Sun 10am–6pm | admission free | Stauffenbergstr. 13 | www.gdw-berlin.de | U 2 Mendelssohn-Bartholdy-Park*

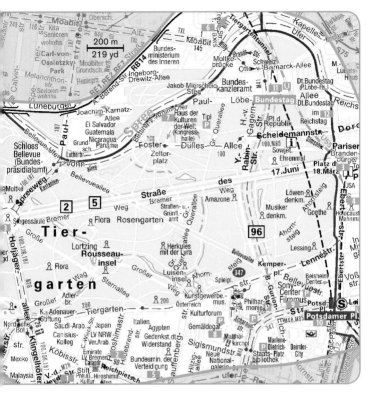

SIGHTSEEING IN TIERGARTEN

1. Bauhaus-Archiv
2. Embassy district
3. Brandenburger Tor
4. Denkmal für die ermordeten Juden Europas
5. Gedenkstätte Deutscher Widerstand
6. Hauptbahnhof (main station)
7. Haus der Kulturen der Welt
8. Kulturforum
9. Mus. für Film und Fernsehen
10. Potsdamer Platz
11. Regierungsviertel
12. Reichstag
13. Siegessäule

6 HAUPTBAHNHOF (151 E1) (*J3*)

One of the largest stations in Europe, it opened in 2006 and was built to designs by the Hamburg architectural practice Gerkan & Partner. Glass and steel are the main elements of the imposing multi-storey building with its many shopping malls and underground tracks running from north to south. More than 1,200 trains pass through here every day; 300,000 passengers and visitors crowd the place. *Europaplatz | U/S Hauptbahnhof*

7 HAUS DER KULTUREN DER WELT (151 E2–3) (*H4*)

This former congress hall was erected for the 1957 Building Exhibition and aroused international interest with its daringly curved roof that led to Berlin residents giving it the nickname of the "pregnant oyster". The building has been used by the Federal Government as the "House of the Cultures of the World" since 1989. Its culture festivals and events focussing on individual countries have underscored its high international reputation. *John-Foster-Dulles-Allee 10 | www.hkw.de | bus 100 Haus der Kulturen der Welt*

⑧ KULTURFORUM (151 E4) (⑪ H5)

All museums: *admission 6–10 euros | www.smb.museum | U/S Potsdamer Platz*
Several of the most important works of European painting from the 13th to 18th centuries are united in the *Gemäldegalerie (Tue–Fri 10am–6pm, Thu until 8pm, Sat/Sun 11am–6pm | Stauffenbergstr. 40)* opened in 1998. The individual artistic landscapes and epochs are presented in 72 main rooms and smaller exhibition spaces with 1,400 works of art. The main focus of the collection is on Italian painting from the 14th to 18th centuries (including works by Caravaggio, Botticelli and Raphael) and 15th and 16th century Dutch art.

Treasures from Baroque art, Delft faïence and Baroque glass are just a few of the highlights displayed in the *Kunstgewerbemuseum (Tue–Fri 10am–6pm, Sat/Sun 11am–6pm | Tiergartenstr. 6)*, also European porcelain – especially Meissen and KPM – decorative utensils and tableware from the Rococo, Classicist and Jugendstil periods, gold and silver articles as well as costumes and silks.

3,300 European musical instruments from the 16th to 21st centuries are in the collection of the *Musikinstrumenten-Museum (Tue–Fri 9am–5pm, Thu until 8pm, Sat/Sun 10am–5pm | Tiergartenstr. 1)*. Among them Carl Maria von Weber's grand piano, a harpsichord that (possibly) once belonged to Johann Sebastian Bach as well as novelties like a walking stick violin. You can even try out some instruments.

20th century European painting and sculpture, from classical modern art to the 1960s, is the main focus of the exhibition in the *Neue Nationalgalerie (closed until 2019 due to reforbishments | Potsdamer Straße 50)* that is housed in a low building designed by Mies van der

TIME TO CHILL

The ● *Liquidrom* **(152 A5)** *(⑪ J5–6) (Sun–Thu 9am–midnight, Fri/Sat 9am–1am | day ticket 29.50 euros | Kreuzberg | Möckernstr. 10 | tel. 030 2 58 00 78 20 | www.liquidrom-berlin.de | U 1, 7 Möckernbrücke)* in the Tempodrom not only scores with its unique architecture. You can float weightlessly in a saltwater tub in a kind of grotto and listen to the dulcet tones of the water that coloured lights turn all colours of the rainbow. In the even-

ing, DJs work the turntables at the edge of the pool – the music ranges from classical to downbeat.
An Oriental Turkish-style steam bath on 1000 m² of space at the ● *Sultan Hamam* **(159 E1)** *(⑪ H6) (Tue–Thu 9:30am–11pm, Fri(Sat 9:30am–midnight women only, Sun family day 11am–10pm | 3 hrs 19 euros | Schöneberg | Bülowstr. 57 | tel. 030 21 75 33 75 | U 2 Bülowstraße)*. Bath towels and slippers can be borrowed.

Roof-covered plaza: Sony Center at the Potsdamer Platz

Rohe. Works by Kirchner, Picasso, Warhol and other masters are on display.

9 MUSEUM FÜR FILM UND FERNSEHEN (140 A6) (*∅ J5*)

The museum exhibits costumes, props, posters, photos, film footage etc. from the beginnings of the German film industry to the modern day. It also focuses on modern film animations, special effects and virtual worlds. In the TV section, you can rediscover old TV series and quiz shows from the last 60 years! *Tue–Sun 10am–6pm, Thu until 8pm | admission 7 euros | Potsdamer Str. 2 | tel. 030 3 00 90 30 | www.deutsche-kinemathek. de | U-/S Potsdamer Platz*

10 POTSDAMER PLATZ ★ (140 A–B6) (*∅ J4*)

This complex in the heart of the city with a shopping centre, cinemas, a musical theatre, casino, hotels and film museum on the west side of Potsdamer Platz was first opened in 1995 – the original buildings on the site were bombed flat during World War II. The tent-like roof Helmut Jahn designed for the ● *Sony Center* is stunning. In every weather, this is the perfect place for people-watching or for simply sitting on one of the café terraces. In the *Kollhoff Tower*, Europe's fastest lift propels visitors up to the ☀ INSIDER TIP viewing platform *(daily 10am–8pm; until 6pm in winter | 6.50 euros)* with a panorama café *(www.panoramapunkt.de)* 93 m (305 ft) above the ground in a mere 20 seconds. *U/S Potsdamer Platz*

11 REGIERUNGSVIERTEL (140 A–B 3–4) (*∅ J4–5*)

To the north of the Reichstag, the Parliament buildings form the so-called "Band des Bundes" – belt of the Federation –, bordered to the west by the *Kanzlerpark* with its helipad and to the east by the *Marie-Elisabeth Lüders* building. This is currently being extended, and alongside offices it also contains the substantial parliamentary library and meeting rooms for the boards of inquiry. The *Bundeskanzleramt* (Federal Chancellery) stands on a bend of the river Spree and was designed by architects Axel Schulte and Charlotte Frank, who also developed the overall concept for the government quarter. The belt is completed by the *Paul-Löbe building,* which houses 21 conference rooms as well as offices for 275 MPs and their staff. Both the Lüders and the Löbe buildings were designed by Stephan Braunfels. The two complexes are separated by a gap that is currently used as a park, but which is earmarked to become the site of a citizens' forum with cafés, galleries and shops – although the plans have been put on ice for some years. Also architecturally interesting: the *Ministergärten* area with its numerous offices housing the official representations of the different German federal states, built between Pariser and Leipziger Platz after the wall came down.

12 REICHSTAG ★
(140 A3–4) (*J4*)

The glass dome, added to the Reichstag building that was originally built by Paul Wallot between 1884 and 1894, has made it a real crowd-puller since the mid-nineties. Visitors have to register in advance with the *Bundestag* for a tour or reserve a table in the *Käfer Restaurant* on the roof if they want to enjoy a walk up the spiral slope inside the 🔅 dome. From up there, you have a fantastic view over the government district, the main railway station and the rest of Berlin, particularly spectacular after nightfall. Down below, members of the German parlia-

Architecture for the 21st century: the office buildings for the members of the Bundestag

ment hold their debates and you can watch them at work through the glass roof.

The Reichstag was set ablaze in 1933 and severely damaged in battles to regain control of Berlin. It was reconstructed between 1961 and 1972 to house an exhibition on German history, now on display in the German Cathedral. After the government's move from Bonn to Berlin was decided in 1991, the building was gutted and crowned with the exciting glass dome after plans by Norman Foster. *Daily 8am–midnight, last admission 10pm; ● free visits to the dome only by appointment (best online) at least 2 hours in advance, also possible on site | Bundestag Visitors' Service (also guided tours and visits to plenary sessions) | Platz der Republik 1 | tel. 030 22 73 21 252 | www.bundestag.de | bus 100 Reichstag*

⊞ SIEGESSÄULE (150 C4) (*ᴔ G4*)

The 67 m (220 ft) high national monument once adorned the square in front of the Reichstag. In order to have more space for his "Reichshauptstadt Germania", Hitler had the golden statue of Victoria – which is affectionately known as "Gold-Else" – moved to the Große Stern in Tiergarten. The Victory Column was designed by Heinrich Strack to commemorate the victory over the Danes and erected between 1864 and 1873. There is a fine view of the city from the 🔍 observation platform. *Daily 9:30am–6:30pm, Nov–March until 5:30pm only | admission 3 euros | Großer Stern | bus 100 Großer Stern*

PRENZLAUER BERG/FRIED-RICHSHAIN

If you like to surround yourself with vegan ice cream, organic cotton clothing and children with trendily old-fashioned names then you will feel right at home here.

The 19th-century historicist buildings in this area – neglected by the GDR as capitalist relics – have long since been restored to their former glory, and the former working-class residents have been replaced by architects, MPs and families leading alternative lifestyles (though without missing out on any creature comforts). There is a high density of bars, restaurants and pubs – though things are a little livelier in *Friedrichshain* than in *Prenzlauer Berg,* where the nightclubs have largely been forced out by neighbours demanding peace and quiet. At the weekend, inhabitants of both areas come together in the *Volkspark Friedrichshain* to skate, go for a stroll or have a barbecue.

◼1 EASTSIDE GALLERY ●
(154 B2) (*N5*)

The largest open-air gallery in the world stretches from the Ostbahnhof to Oberbaum Bridge. 118 artists have immortalised themselves here on 1,316 m (4,318 ft) of Berlin Wall. The best-known works are "My God, Help Me To Survive This Deadly Love" by Dmitri Vrubel and Gerhard Lahr's "Berlin–New York". *Friedrichshain | Mühlenstraße | www.east sidegallery.com | U/S Ostbahnhof*

◼2 INSIDER TIP ERNST-THÄLMANN-PARK (147 F4) (*N2*)

One of the few locations where GDR-era buildings haven't been expunged from the city. This residential estate with its high-rise blocks opened in 1986 on Greifswalder Straße, and was intended as a template for how all GDR citizens would ultimately be housed. Today, the complex is listed – including an enormous memorial to Ernst Thälmann himself. *Prenzlauer Berg | S Greifswalder Straße*

◼3 KOLLWITZPLATZ
(147 D4–5) (*L–M2*)

Avoiding destruction almost completely, this ensemble of houses around the square is one of the loveliest groups of historical buildings in Berlin. The square was named after the painter and graphic artist Käthe Kollwitz who lived here with her husband from 1891 to 1943. In a small park, a monument created by the sculptor Gustav Seitz in 1958 acts as a memorial to the famous resident. Kollwitzplatz is also known for its weekly market *(Thu noon–7pm, Sat 9am–4pm)* and its many cafés and restaurants. *Prenzlauer Berg | U 2 Senefelderplatz*

◼4 KULTURBRAUEREI (147 D4) (*L2*)

The former Schultheiss Brewery has established itself as a cultural centre with a cinema, clubs and shops. Since 2013, there's also the interesting INSIDER TIP exhibition of everyday culture of the GDR *(Tue–Sun 10am–6pm, Thu 10am–8pm | free admission)*. The building, constructed in yellow brick that is so typical of Berlin, was erected between 1890 and 1910 to plans drawn up by the royal architect Franz Schwechten who also designed the Kaiser Wilhelm Memorial Church. *Prenzlauer Berg | Knaackstr. 75–97 | U 2 Eberswalder Straße*

◼5 MAUERPARK
(146 C3–4) (*K–L 1–2*)

Many dogs and many more adults and children have a great time in this park on

Buskers in Friedrichshain

Krossener Str

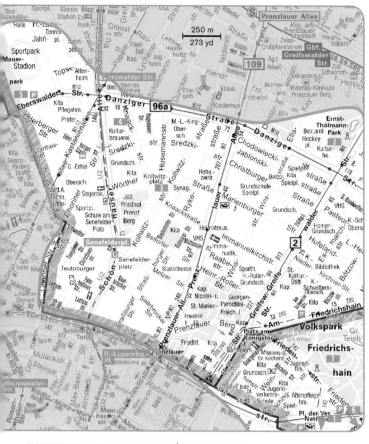

SIGHTSEEING IN PRENZLAUER BERG/FRIEDRICHSHAIN

1 Eastside Gallery
2 Ernst-Thälmann-Park
3 Kollwitzplatz
4 Kulturbrauerei
5 Mauerpark
6 Oberbaumbrücke
7 Volkspark Friedrichshain

what used to be the border between East and West Berlin. Today, graffiti artists try out their talents on a remaining piece of the Wall. The highlights are the gigantic swings to the south and the children's farm at the north end. On Sundays in summer karaoke shows and the large fleamar-

ket pull the crowds. *Prenzlauer Berg | Eberswalder Str. | U 2 Eberswalder Straße*

6 OBERBAUMBRÜCKE
(154 B2) (*ω N5*)

The bridge with its elevated railway tracks, street and covered walkway over the

Spree unites Friedrichshain and Kreuzberg. It is considered a masterpiece of 19th century architecture and was constructed for a trade exhibition in 1896. The name "Oberbaum", "upper barrier", comes from the days when customs officials blocked shipping lanes here with a barrier so that they could collect their tolls. The Spanish architect Santiago Calatrava designed the new middle section when the bridge was renovated in the 1990s. *Friedrichshain | U1 Schlesisches Tor*

⑦ VOLKSPARK FRIEDRICHSHAIN
(153 F1) (*ℳ M–N3*)

The 128-acre Volkspark Friedrichshain i is where people go to race their skateboards through the half-pipe while their parents and younger brothers and sisters relax near the ● INSIDER TIP *Märchenbrunnen*. Not only children love this fountain that was first filled with water in 1913; arches frame stone bowls with cascades and characters from Grimm's fairy tales. An open-air cinema at the park's east side attracts visitors to the park at night in summer. You can also enjoy a Pils in the beer garden or coffee and cake in its restaurant *(www.schoenbrunn.net | Moderate)* at the park's Schwanenteich (swan pond). As for the rest: meadowsfor picnics, football etc.*Friedrichshain | bus 142, 200 Am Friedrichshain*

KREUZBERG

Kreuzberg is where Turkish people rub shoulders with bearded hipsters and university professors housed in spacious apartments: a rich blend of cultures and lifestyles.

Before the fall of the wall, the area was home to immigrant workers and military service-dodgers from West Germany. The latter established an alternative scene that continues to the present day in the form of a lively mix of cafés, bars and clubs,

The Oberbaumbrücke connects Kreuzberg and Friedrichshain

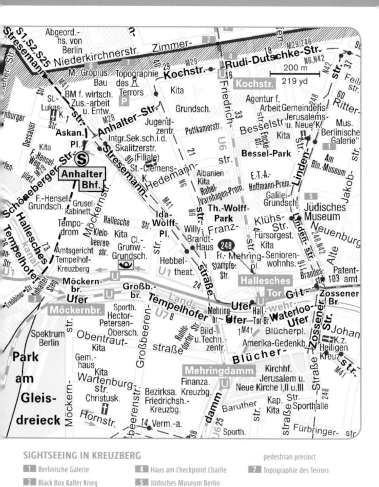

SIGHTSEEING IN KREUZBERG

1 Berlinische Galerie
2 Black Box Kalter Krieg
3 Deutsches Technikmuseum
4 Haus am Checkpoint Charlie
5 Jüdisches Museum Berlin
6 Martin-Gropius-Bau

pedestrian precinct
7 Topographie des Terrors

and is now accompanied by Turkish and Arab bakeries, cultural associations and bridal shops. All residents come together at the weekly market on Maybachufer *(Tue, Fri 11am–6pm)*. Well-to-do academics treat themselves to fancy apartments around Bergmannstraße, while the seedy Kottbusser Tor constantly hits the head-lines due to its drug-related crime. The biggest party spot can be found at night around Schlesisches Tor.

1 INSIDER TIP BERLINISCHE GALERIE
(152 C5) (∅ K5)
You will be dazzled by the works of the so-called "Neue Wilden" that evolved

around Rainer Fetting, and those of the "old"Expressionists in the State Gallery for Modern Art, photography and architecture. New Realism is represented with works by Otto Dix and George Grosz. Special exhibitions. *Wed–Mon 10am–6pm | admission 8 euros | Alte Jakobstr. 124–28 | www.berlinischegalerie.de | U 1, 6, 15 Hallesches Tor*

2 BLACK BOX KALTER KRIEG
(152 B4) (*M K5*)

A 240 square yards big black information box documents the recent German history: starting with the allied victory, followed by the armament and ending with the fall of the communist regime. A map shows the division of Berlin into four sectors by the victorious powers. *Daily 10am–6pm | admission 5 euros | Friedrichstr. 47/corner of Zimmermannstr. | www.bfgg.de/zentrum-kalter-krieg | U 6 Kochstraße*

The Jüdische Museum also tracks the fates of individuals

3 DEUTSCHES TECHNIKMUSEUM
(151 F6) (*M J6*)

Young and old will be delighted by this collection of historical vehicles, instruments and inventions. You will really need more than a day if you want to visit the engine shed with its historic locomotives and the shipping section with 1,500 exhibits. In *Spectrum (Möckernstr. 26)* 150 experiments explain technical principles. The INSIDER TIP permanent exhibition "The Network" takes visitors on a discovery tour through our networked reality. *Tue–Fri 9am–5:30pm, Sat/Sun 10am–6pm | admission 8 euros | Trebbiner Str. 9 | www.sdtb.de | U 1, 2 Gleisdreieck*

4 HAUS AM CHECKPOINT CHARLIE
(140 C6) (*M K5*)

Permanent exhibition on the construction of the Wall and division of the city. Documentation of attempts to escape and the vehicles used for this: from mini-submarines to a hot-air balloon. *Daily 9am–10pm | admission 12.50 euros | Friedrichstr. 43 | www.mauer-museum.com | U 6 Kochstraße*

5 JÜDISCHES MUSEUM BERLIN ★
(152 B–C5) (*M K5*)

The permanent exhibition in the spectacular building designed by the New York architect Daniel Libeskind that is connected to the old Baroque building shows 2,000 years of Jewish culture. Multimedia technology, lighting effects and the unorthodox layout of the exhibition rooms create an emotional connection between the visitors and exhibits. One of the many subjects dealt with is the history of the persecution of Jews in Germany from the early Middle Ages to the present day. The glass plaza was created in 2007 by roofing over the former central courtyard. *Mon 10am–10pm, Tue–Sun 10am–8pm | admission 8 euros |*

Lindenstr. 9–14 | www.jmberlin.de | U 1, 6, 15 Hallesches Tor

⑥ MARTIN-GROPIUS-BAU
(152 A4) (⌘ J5)

Originally a museum for arts and crafts, this magnificent building with its beautiful reliefs and mosaics which was erected between 1877 and 1881 to plans drawn up by Martin Gropius (Walter Gropius' great-uncle) and Heino Schmieden, now serves as an atmospheric location for contemporary art, photography and history exhibitions. *Wed–Mon 10am–7pm | different admission fees for the various exhibitions | Niederkirchner Str. 7 | www.gropiusbau.de | S 1, 25 Anhalter Bahnhof*

⑦ TOPOGRAPHIE DES TERRORS
(152 A4) (⌘ J5)

An open-air exhibition on the site of the former centre of power of the National Socialist, SS police state provides information on the atrocities that were planned and organised here. The outdoor area next to Martin Gropius-Bau is home to a display featuring sections of the wall of the prison courtyard and the Berlin wall – as well as a programme of temporary exhibitions. *Daily 10am–8pm | free admission | guided tours by appointment | Niederkirchner Str. 8 | www.topographie.de | S 1, 25 Anhalter Bahnhof*

CHARLOTTEN-BURG/WIL-MERSDORF

Shopping district, gourmet quarter and culture – all of this is concentrated in the districts of Charlottenburg between KaDeWe and Schloss Charlottenburg, and Wilmersdorf to the south of Ku'damm.

The number of restaurants around Savignyplatz must break all records, while the palace gardens are teeming with joggers and museum visitors. Kurfürstendamm is still the traditional shopping strip for the better-heeled, while the younger crowd gather in the shade of the Memorial Church and shop in the new designer shop centre Bikini-Haus. With the Theater des Westens, Schaubühne, German Opera and Schiller Theatre, Charlottenburg competes with the theatres in the east of the city. Wilmersdorf attracts people with its numerous traditional, speciality shops.

① C/O BERLIN (139 D4) (⌘ F5)

The place to go for contemporary photography in Berlin, C/O Berlin has been staging a series of temporary exhibitions ever since it moved into the Amerika Haus in 2014. This architectural gem was built in the 1950s as an intercultural centre, and later became a focal point of demonstrations against the Vietnam war. *Daily 11am–8pm | admission 10 euros | Charlottenburg | Hardenbergstr. 22–24 | www.co-berlin.org | U/S Zoologischer Garten*

② FUNKTURM (148 B5) (⌘ C5)

Modelled on the Eiffel Tower in Paris, but considerably smaller, the Berlin counterpart was erected on the Fair grounds in 1926 and was considered the modern landmark of Berlin for many years. Especially in the divided city the 138 m (453 ft) "beanpole" – as the locals called it – became a symbol for the inhabitants of West Berlin. There is a restaurant 55 m (180 ft) above ground level and a 📷 viewing platform 71 m (233 ft) feet higher up. The transmission mast at the top of the tower is used for the police radio. As the tower is often closed for servicing, it is wise to call before you make a visit. *Mon 10am–8pm, Tue–Sun 10am–11pm | admission 5 euros |*

CHARLOTTENBURG/WILMERSDORF

Charlottenburg | Messedamm 22 | tel. 030 30 38 19 05 | www.funkturm-messeberlin. de | S 7, 41, 42 Messe Nord | U 2 Kaiserdamm

3 KAISER-WILHELM-GEDÄCHTNIS-KIRCHE (139 E4) *(⌘ G5)*

The bleak ruins of the tower of the church erected between 1891 and 1895 on Breitscheidplatz in memory of Kaiser Wilhelm I point into the sky like a warning finger. After it was almost completely destroyed in World War II, church officials decided to at least leave its tower standing. Between 1958 and 1961 a modern octagonal church constructed of 16,000 blue glass bricks, designed by Egon Eiermann, was erected adjacent to it. There is an exhibition on the history of the church on the ground floor of the tower. *Daily 9am–7pm, Memorial Hall Mon–Fri 10am–6pm, Sat 10am–5:30pm, Sun noon–5:30pm, church concert Sat 6pm | Charlottenburg | Kurfürstendamm 237 | www.gedaechtnis kirche-berlin.de | U/S Zoologischer Garten*

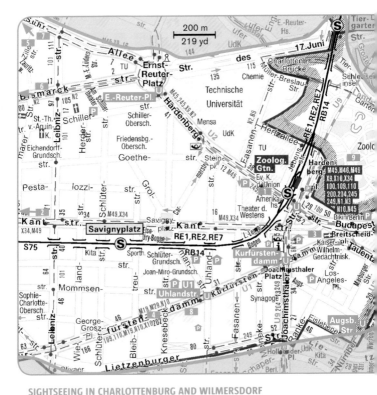

SIGHTSEEING IN CHARLOTTENBURG AND WILMERSDORF

- **1** C/O Berlin
- **2** Funkturm
- **3** Kaiser-Wilh.-Gedächtniskirche
- **4** Kurfürstendamm
- **5** Museum Berggruen
- **6** Olympia Stadium
- **7** Schloss Charlottenburg
- **8** The Story of Berlin
- **9** Zoologischer Garten

4 KURFÜRSTENDAMM ●
(149 D–F6) (*∅ D–F 5–6*)

Before reunification, this shopping boulevard was the epitome of (West) Berlin's metropolitan flair. Recently, many eyesores from the 1960s have been demolished and architectural treasures like the *Zoopalast* cinema and the *Bikini-Haus* have been renovated which lures young people back to the shopping mile. The boulevard was laid out as a 3.5 km (2 miles) ride between 1883 and 1886 and some houses still bear witness to the opulent turn-of-the-century architecture around 1900. *Charlottenburg | U 1, 9 Kurfürstendamm*

5 MUSEUM BERGGRUEN
(148 C3) (*∅ D4*)

Works by Picasso and Paul Klee form the core of this collection assembled by the art dealer Heinz Berggruen. Early works, as well as paintings, sculptures and works on paper, are exhibited under the title "Picasso and his Time" on three floors in this magnificent building designed by Stüler. Beautiful sculpture garden. *Tue–Fri 10am–6pm, Sat/Sun 11am–6pm | admission 10 euros | Charlottenburg | Schlossstr. 1 | www.smb.museum | S 41, 42 Westend*

6 OLYMPIA STADIUM
(164 C3) (*∅ A–B4*)

Designed by Werner March, the stadium was opened for the 1936 Olympic Games, making it part of the propaganda machine with which the Nazis presented themselves to the world. Nowadays, it is home to the professional footballers at Hertha BSC. The stadium which holds 75,000 people was completely renovated for the 2006 Football World Championship. All seats are now protected from the weather. *Daily 9am–7pm, in winter 10am–4pm, Aug 9am–8pm | tours of the stadium daily 11am, April–Oct also 1pm, 3pm, Aug also 5pm, except when Hertha*

Gedächtniskirche with the modern extension designed by Egon Eiermann

BSC is playing or other events are on | admission without tour guide 7 euros, including guide 11 euros | Charlottenburg | Olympischer Platz 3 | tel. 030 25 00 23 22 | www.olympiastadion-berlin.de | U 2 Olympiastadion

7 SCHLOSS CHARLOTTENBURG ★
(148–149 C–D 2–3) (*∅ D4*)

The more than 300-year-old summer residence of the Electress Sophie Charlotte impresses with its grand architecture from the 17th and 18th centuries. The apartments of Friedrich I and his wife are open to the public. The mausoleum of Queen Luise, the wife of Friedrich Wilhelm III, is at the far end of the park. Due to refurbishments, varying areas are not accessible. *Old Palace April–Oct Tue–Sun 10am–6pm*

(Nov–March until 5pm), New Wing April–Oct Tue–Sun 10am–6pm (Nov–March until 5pm), Belvedere (KPM Porcelain Collection) and Mausoleum April–Oct Tue–Sun 10am–6pm, New Pavilion (art and crafts of the Romantic movement) Tue–Sun 10am–5pm, in summer until 6pm | admission: joint ticket 12 euros, otherwise Old and New Wing 10 euros, Belvedere 4 euros, New Pavilion 4 euros, Mausoleum 2 euros | Charlottenburg | Spandauer Damm 10–22 | www.spsg.de | bus 145 Luisenplatz

8 THE STORY OF BERLIN
(150 A6) (*ꝒꝒ F5*)

Going around the 24 rooms will seem like a journey through time during which you will find out a great deal about the history of Berlin. Young people in particular will be fascinated by all the hi-tech and multimedia installations. *Daily 10am–8pm, last admission 6pm | admission 12 euros | Charlottenburg | Kurfürstendamm 207 | www.story-of-berlin.de | U 1 Uhlandstraße*

9 ZOOLOGISCHER GARTEN
(139 E–F 3–4) (*ꝒꝒ F–G5*)

The 170-year-old zoo is the oldest in Germany and – with its 18,600 animals of 1,400 species – the most diverse in the world. Just one highlight: the old-fashioned ● *aquarium* with the crocodile section. *Daily 9am–6:30pm, until 4:30pm in winter | admission 14.50 euros, with aquarium 20 euros | Charlottenburg | Budapester Str. 5 | www.zoo-berlin.de | U/S Zoologischer Garten*

IN OTHER DISTRICTS

ALLIIERTENMUSEUM (162 B3) (*ꝒꝒ C9*)

In the heart of the former American sector, the subject is the history of the western powers and Berlin in the years from 1945 to 1994. There is an impressive documentation of the Berlin Airlift in 1948/49 and you can even inspect one of the planes the local residents called "raisin bombers" parked outside. In the long run, the museum is expected to relocate to the former Tempelhof airport (see *Tempelhofer Feld, p. 60*). *Tue–Sun 10am–6pm | free admission | Zehlendorf | Clayallee 135 | www.alliiertenmuseum.de | U 3 Oskar-Helene-Heim*

INSIDER TIP ▶ BERLINER UNTERWELTEN
(146 A2) (*ꝒꝒ K1*)

The guided tours offered by the Berliner Unterwelten association are not for the faint-hearted, as they take visitors through the subterranean world beneath the city on the hunt for hidden traces of its past. Bunkers from the Second World War and the Cold War are still preserved, as are the remnants of escape tunnels dug beneath the wall from both the east and the west. For something a little more relaxed, try the tour through the former Kindl brewery in Neukölln, which also comes with a basic course in German brewing. Sturdy shoes are recommended, and a minimum age limit applies to some of the tours. *Daily guided tours | schedule: www.berliner-unterwelten.de | from 11 euros | tickets at the underground station Gesundbrunnen | Brunnenstr. 105*

BOTANISCHER GARTEN ●
(163 E2–3) (*ꝒꝒ E9–10*)

The whole natural world can be found on this 1,070-acre site: Siberian steppe grass, Japanese cherry trees and common or garden vegetables located in a spacious park in Steglitz. Highlights include the huge old buildings housing tropical plants, giant water-lilies, bamboo and palm trees; the orchid hall and cactus collection are also superb. *Daily 9am to nightfall | admission 6 euros |*

The big splash: in the hippo hall of the Berlin Zoo

Dahlem | Königin-Luise-Str. 6–8 | second entrance: Steglitz | Unter den Eichen | www.bgbm.org | S 1 Botanischer Garten

BRÜCKE-MUSEUM (162 B1) (*C8*)

This idyllically located building in Grunewald houses an impressive collection of works by those artists who came together in Dresden in 1905 to form the "Brücke" (Bridge) group including Ernst Ludwig Kirchner, Erich Heckel, Karl Schmitt-Rottluff, Max Pechstein and Emil Nolde. *Wed–Mon 11am–5pm | admission 6 euros | Dahlem | Bussardsteig 9 | www.bruecke-museum.de | bus 115 Pücklerstraße*

GÄRTEN DER WELT (165 E3) (*0*)

For over 30 years now, the *Gärten der Welt* ("Gardens of the World") have been showcasing examples of the horticultural arts from across China, Japan, the Far East and Europe on a 20-hectare site. Thanks to the International Garden Exhibition of 2017, they have recently added new features such as an English garden and a cable car

connecting the Gärten der Welt with the newly built garden park on the Kienberg, where you can climb a futuristic ⚡ lookout platform. Inside the gardens themselves, we recommend taking part in a relaxing ● tea ceremony in the *Berghaus zum Osmanthussaft (8 euros | reservations: tel. 0179 3 94 55 64). Daily from 9am to nightfall | admission 5 euros | Marzahn | Eisenacher Str. 99 | www.gruen-berlin.de | U 5 Cottbusser Platz, then Bus 195 Erholungspark Marzahn*

GEDENKSTÄTTE HOHEN-SCHÖNHAUSEN (165 E3) (*Q2*)

Here, in the middle of a residential zone, is where the GDR leadership used to lock up their political prisoners behind high walls and barbed wire. As you tour the facility, you will hear eyewitness accounts of the inhuman methods which the system used to try to crush the spirits of its opponents. There is also a free exhibition where you can learn about the victims' experiences. *Guided tours Mon–Fri 11am,*

1pm, 3pm, March–Oct also 10am, noon, 2pm, 4pm, Sat/Sun hourly 10am–4pm | admission 6 euros | Hohenschönhausen | Genslerstr. 66 | tel. 030 98 60 82 30 | www.stiftung-hsh.de | tram 6 Genslerstraße

GRUNEWALD
(156 A5–6, 162 A–B 1–2) (𝄞 A–C 5–10)

When the city was divided by the Wall, Grunewald as West Berlin's largest forested area was the epitome of a recreation area. Today, it is much more peaceful. Several lakes including *Teufelssee* (Devil's Lake) as well as the River Havel will tempt you to take a swim. Teufelssee is also the site of ⊛ *Ökowerk (tel. 030 3 00 50)* which offers a natural garden, beehives and survival courses for children. The 16th century *Jagdschloss Grunewald (April–Oct Tue–Sun 10am–6pm, Nov/Dec Sat/Sun 10am–4pm | admission 6 euros)* on the banks of Lake Grunewald has a beautiful Renaissance hall, a valuable collection of paintings and a hunting museum. The 120 m (394 ft) high *Teufelsberg* (Devil's Mountain) in the north was created from the mass of rubble from buildings destroyed during the war. *Grunewald | S 7, 9 Grunewald*

HOUSE OF THE WANNSEE CONFERENCE (164 B4) (𝄞 0)

On 20 January 1942, representatives of the Nazi regime and the SS met in this mansion with a view of the lake to finalise the organisation of the genocide of the Jews based on a decision that had been made previously. An exhibition on the ground floor provides information on the conference, the events leading up to it and its horrific consequences. *Daily 10am–6pm | free admission | Wannsee | Am Großen Wannsee 56–58 | tel. 030 805 00 10 | www.ghwk.de | S Wannsee, then bus 114 Haus der Wannseekonferenz*

JÜDISCHER FRIEDHOF WEISSENSEE (165 D3) (𝄞 O–P 1–2)

The cemetery, which was established in 1880, is one of the largest and most beautiful Jewish graveyards in Europe. The brick building and layout of the burial areas were designed by Hugo Licht. A memorial stone has been erected in remembrance of the 6 million Jews who were murdered by the National Socialists. The publishers Samuel Fischer and Rudolf Mosse, as well as the painter Lesser Ury, are among the prominent people buried

FLOATING SWIMMING POOL

Hopefully, you've brought your bikini or swimming trunks, otherwise you'll miss out on this urban summer fun: Since 2004 the hull of a barge filled with water has been used as a floating swimming pool on the Spree. The water doesn't come from the river but from the tap. The walls of the ship have been lined with blue plastic like any other swimming pool. When it's sunny, the jetties and beach nearby the *Badeschiff* **(154 B5) (𝄞 O6)** are bursting with party people. In the evenings, DJs work the turntables. On summer weekends it is often so full that it can take a while before you get a turn to jump into Berlin's biggest bath tub. They also offer courses like yoga, massages and stand-up paddleboarding. *May–Sept daily 8am–midnight | day ticket 5.50 euros | Treptow | Eichenstr. 4 | tel. 0162 5 45 13 74 | www. arena-berlin.de | S Treptower Park*

Swim with a view: the floating swimming pool at the Osthafen

here. Men must wear a head covering (can be borrowed at the entrance). *April–Oct Sun–Thu 7:30am–5pm, Fri 7:30am–2:30pm, Nov–March until 4pm, Fri until 2:30pm | Weißensee | Herbert-Baum-Str. 45 | tram 12 Albertinenstraße*

PFAUENINSEL ● (164 B4) (*ØØ 0*)

Originally, the 165-acre Pfaueninsel (Peacock Island) was the site of the zoo that Friedrich Wilhelm III had set up at the beginning of the 19th century. Today, only the peacocks in the wild and the romantic park are a reminder of the island's original purpose. The little white castle looks like a film set. It was built for Wilhelmine Enke, the paramour of Friedrich Wilhelm II. Take a look at the *dairy* and the hall in the style of a Gothic Revival church where parties were held. *Castle: April–Oct Tue–Sun 10am–5:30pm, guided tours only, admission 6 euros; dairy: April–Oct Sat/Sun 10am–5:30pm, admission 2 euros | Wannsee | Pfaueninselchaussee | ferry daily all year | 4 euros | www.spsg.de | tel. 030 80 58 68 31 | bus 218 Pfaueninsel*

INSIDER TIP RIXDORF (165 D4) (*ØØ N8*)

This small village with its sheds and forges, once founded by the Bohemians, is situated in the middle of the Neukölln mass of houses. Here you get a feeling of how the Berlin metropolis once grew out of many small locations. Pretty: the Bohemian Bethlehem Church and the Bohemian Cemetery. *U 7 Karl-Marx-Straße*

SOWJETISCHES EHRENMAL (155 D4) (*ØØ P7*)

One of the largest Soviet military cemeteries in Germany is located in Treptow Park. Not only the grave slabs in memory of the 7,000 Soviet soldiers who fell in the Battle of Berlin are impressive, the sheer size of the complex is also astonishing: eight walls with reliefs, the monumental 12 m (49 ft) high bronze sculpture of a soldier carrying a rescued German child, as well as the gigantic sculpture "Mother Homeland" that was chiselled out of a 50-ton block of granite. The monument was erected between 1947 and 1949. *Treptow | Alt-Treptow 1 | S Treptower Park*

Socialist pathos: Soviet memorial in Treptower Park

TEMPELHOFER FELD ★ ●
(160–161 B–E 3–6) (*ᗩ K–M 7–9*)

Even today Europe's biggest office building, the central building of the *Tempelhof airport,* with a length of 1,300 yd and 5,000 rooms, gives an impression of the monumental architecture of the National Socialism. Opened in 1936 for the Olympic Games in Berlin, an international flying hub and the seat for the air ministry were planned. This airport is no longer in use since 2008. The site is to be kept as a recreational space for the long term; it is used during the day by joggers, skaters and walkers. At the moment, refugees are also housed here. Segways can be hired at the site's west entrance (Tempelhofer Damm) and small allotments have been created at the east end (urban gardening). On *Platz der Luftbrücke* a monument pays homage to the Berin Airlift during the soviet Berlin blockade 1948/49. *Park daily from sunrise to nightfall | free admission | guided tours of the buildings Mon–Fri 4pm, Fri also 1pm, Sat/Sun noon, 3pm | 15 euros| Tempelhof | Platz der Luftbrücke | www.tempelhoferfreiheit. de | U 6 Platz der Luftbrücke*

TIERPARK FRIEDRICHSFELDE
(165 E3) (*ᗩ S5–6*)

Enjoy this spacious zoo which houses around 7,500 animals of over 800 species, located in what was once a castle park designed by the famous landscape architect Peter Joseph Lenné. Highlights include the walk-in Vari-Wald (lemurs from Madagascar), the walk-in kangaroo compound and the bathing elephants on weekends. The early Classicist *Friedrichsfelde Castle (Tue, Thu, Sat, Sun 11am–5pm)* from 1690 can be visited; concerts are frequently held in the main hall. *Daily 9am–6:30pm, until 4:30pm in winter | admission 13 euros | Lichtenberg | Am Tierpark 125 | www.tierpark-berlin.de | tel. 030 51 53 10 | U 5 Tierpark*

EXCURSIONS

KÖPENICK (165 E4) (*m 0*)

In the German-speaking world, this waterside town to the south-east of Berlin is known due to a story about a bogus captain who confiscated the city's treasury in 1906. Köpenick has been part of Greater Berlin since 1920 but has managed to preserve its own charm. Along with its pretty old town and castle, Müggelsee is the perfect destination for a relaxing day trip away from city life.

The best way to get to Köpenick is on the water. In summer, boats run by the *Stern- und Kreisschifffahrt (www.sternundkreis. de)* leave Treptow harbour every hour. The excursion boats take 60 minutes to steam upstream along the Spree, past the industrial complexes of former East Germany, the Plänter Forest and idyllic shoreline properties. Visitors for Köpenick should disembark at Am Luisenhain in the heart of the old town. The famous red-brick *town hall* is directly opposite. In 1906, one year after it was opened, the unemployed shoemaker WilhelmVoigt decided to gain entry into the town hall wearing a captain's uniform, arrest the mayor and steal the borough's coffers. An exhibition in the town hall *(Mon–Fri 9am–6pm, Sat/Sun 9am–5pm | admission free)* documents the story that inspired the author Carl Zuckmayer to write his famous play "The Captain of Köpenick". A bronze statue commemorates him at the town hall entrance.

The magnificent and beautifully restored *Köpenicker Schloss*, a moated 17th century castle, is located around 200 m (655 ft) to the south of the town hall and was originally built for the later King Friedrich I of Prussia. It houses the *Kunstgewerbemuseum (Tue–Sun 10am–6pm | admission 6 euros)* with an exhibition of historical craftsmanship. The castle park, with its delightful café, is an ideal place

FIT IN THE CITY

Aspria Spa & Sports **(149 D6)** *(m D5)* *(Mon–Fri 6am–11pm, Sat 8am–10pm | day ticket 27–85 euros | Charlottenburg | Karlsruher Str. 20 | tel. 030 8 90 68 88 60 | www.aspria-berlin.de | U 7 Adenauerplatz)*) is a fantastic fitness and wellness temple spread over 16,000 m². 25 m/82 ft pool and a wide range of courses even for day visitors as well as a children's sport programme and sauna. At its opening in 1930, the *Stadtbad Mitte* **(146 B6)** *(m K3)* *(Mon–Wed 6:30am–10pm, Thu until 2pm, Fri noon–10pm, Sat 2pm–9:30pm | admission 3.50–5.50 euros depending on the time of day | Gartenstr. 5 | tel. 030*

30 88 09 12 | www.berlinerbaeder.de | S 1, 2, 25 Nordbahnhof) was Europe's most modern swimming pool and is still popular with fast swimmers. Behind a 10 m/33 ft high glass front and under a glass-covered roof, the pool is 50 m/164 ft long and the water stays at a pleasant 28 degrees Celsius.

Jogging around the city: sport enthusiasts can practise their hobby along the Spree and manage the distance from the Reichstag to Schloss Charlottenburg (9 km/5.6miles) – and back by cruise ship! Nice jogging routes can also be found in Tiergarten, Grunewald and on the Tempelhofer Feld.

to take a break with a view of *Frauentog*, a bay on the River Dahme. Here you'll find the ◉ *Solarbootpavillon (March–Oct Mon–Fri noon–7pm, Sat/Sun 10am–7pm, during the summer holidays daily 10am–7pm | tel. 0160 6 30 99 97 | www.solar-waterworld.de):* This is where you can rent a solar-boat from 10 euros an hour and glide silently over the Spree and Dahme. From your boat you will be able to see the *Fischerkietz* (Fisherman's District) – a lovely settlement with historical fishermen's houses and the *Flussbad Gartenstraße (Mon–Sat 1pm–6pm | admission 3 euros)* – on the eastern shore of the Frauentog.

Excursion boats sail on further from the Luisenhain dock to *Müggelsee*. You can also reach Berlin's largest lake by tram (lines 60 and 61 in the direction of "Altes Wasserwerk") in around 20 minutes. Get off at the Müggelseedamm/Bölschestraße stop and walk about 300 m (984 ft) to the lake with its beer garden, beach bar and small – but first-rate – French restaurant *Domaines (www.domaines-berlin.de | Moderate)*. The Spreetunnel leads to the west shore of the lake where there are several places to go swimming. A stroll along the lakeside will take you to the popular, rustic *Rübezahl* inn. During summer, ships depart from here for Friedrichshagen. The quickest way back to the centre of Berlin is then by district line from Friedrichshagen station. Information: *Tourist information Köpenick (Mon–Fri 9am–6pm, Sat 10am–4pm, in winter only until 1pm on Saturdays | Alt-Köpenick 31–33 | Am Schlossplatz | tel. 030 65 57 55 01 | www.berlin-tourismus-online.de)*

POTSDAM (164 B4–5) (*∅ 0*)

The capital of Brandenburg attracts many visitors with its chic villas, magnificent castle grounds and Prussian history. It is located to the south-west of Berlin on the opposite bank of the Havel and can be easily reached on the district line *(line 7, every 10 minutes).*

Today, what used to be the royal seat of the Prussian kings is a town with a unique cultural and park landscape. Since 1990, large sections of Potsdam have been declared a Unesco World Heritage Site. These include Sanssouci park, the Neuer Garten, Babelsberg and Glienicke (on the Berlin side of the Havel) with their respective castles. ★ *Schloss Sanssouci* park is a magnificent example of French and Italian landscape garden architecture. The *Expressbus X 15 (mid-April–Oct., in winter bus 695)* will take you to the park from Potsdam-Stadt station where the district line from Berlin arrives; get off at the Schloss Sanssouci stop. Originally, the park was only a terraced garden that Friedrich II (the Great) had laid out in 1744 to cultivate fruit and wine. He then fell in love with the view from the hill to such an extent that he had a palace built above the terraces as his summer residence. The single-storey palace, barely 100 m (328 ft) long, was constructed by Georg Wenzeslaus von Knobelsdorff in a mere two years (1745–47). Schloss Sanssouci (which means "without a care") is relatively small and was intended to serve the young king as a place where he could relax. This is where the king spent his summers studying philosophy, music and literature and receiving guests.

Friedrich II had several other buildings, including the *Neue Palais* and the *Chinesisches Teehaus*, erected in addition to the palace. The *Neue Palais* was the last and, at the same time, largest 18th century construction project in the park at Sanssouci. It was built for Friedrich the Great between 1763 and 1769 to show that he had not been financially ruined by the Silesian wars. A stroll through the park will

Fruit and wine used to be grown on the terraced gardens at Schloss Sanssouci

take you past the *Orangery* and several gardens devoted to specific themes.

A 15-minute, signposted, walk from the park exit leads you back to town. The **INSIDER TIP** *Holländisches Viertel*, erected for Dutch immigrants between 1732 and 1742, is located at Nauener Tor. The soldier-king Friedrich Wilhelm I recruited them as he needed well-trained craftsmen to carry out extensions to his garrison city. Today "Little Amsterdam" is popular for its mixture of shops and pubs. The Russian colony *Alexandrowka*, with 14 small, decorated wooden houses from the early 19th century, is located to the north of the Dutch Quarter. This is where the Russian singers the Tsar had given to King Friedrich Wilhelm II as a present were housed.

Bus 692 from Nauener Tor will take you to *Schloss Cecilienhof (April–Oct Tue–Sun 10am–6pm, Nov–March Tue–Sun 10am–5pm)* where the Potsdam Conference was held by the Allies in 1945. The palace includes an exhibition on the conference.

Cecilienhof was constructed between 1914 and 1917 in style of an English country house for Crown Prince Wilhelm and his wife Cecilie; it was the last palace built by the Hohenzollern family.

Another attraction is the *Neue Garten* around Schloss Cecilienhof, an English-style landscape garden at the Heiligen See where you can swim in summer. A sight for sore eyes is the *Marmorpalais (Nov–March Sat/ Sun 10am–4pm, until 6pm in April, May–Oct Tue–Sun 10am–6pm | admission 6 euros)* on the bank which Friedrich Wilhelm II. had built between 1787–92. The architects were Carl von Gontard and, from 1789, Carl Gotthard Langhans who also designed the Brandenburger Tor. Information*: Tourist Information (April–Oct Mon–Fri 9:30am–6pm, Sat/Sun 9:30am–4pm, Nov–March Mon–Fri 9:30am–6pm | Luisenplatz 3 | tel. 0331 27 55 88 99 | www.potsdam.de) and in the main railway station (Mon–Sat 9:30am–8pm, in the winter until 6pm)*

FOOD & DRINK

Berlin is a gourmet's paradise. There is a wide choice of places to eat ranging from internationally acclaimed restaurants with Michelin stars to organic raw-food cuisine and the legendary curry-wurst, there is something here to suit literally every taste.

The times when Berlin's cuisine consisted solely of meatballs, pickled eggs and turnips are long gone, and for many residents, food is an important part of their lifestyle. Whether their customers follow a vegan diet, imitate their Stone-Age forebears by eating paleo and avoiding sugar and grains, or believe that their food should be grown organically – the restaurants always adapt to follow the latest trend. Especially in central districts such as Mitte, Friedrichshain and Kreuzberg, you can enjoy modern food that draws inspiration from every corner of the globe, and that tastes a lot better than you might otherwise expect from organic, vegan fare.

Alongside all this healthy eating and environmental awareness, the city's menus also reflect Berlin's internationalism. Vietnamese and Indian restaurants offer cheap and tasty grub on every street corner, and if you're in a hurry you can pick up a doner kebab or a falafel sandwich from one of the countless food stands – often for as little as 3 euros. The curry-wurst – which Berliners claim was invented here – also has its place on the menu, though anyone looking for something quick but not necessarily deep-fried can pick up a sandwich or bagel from one

Photo: Desserts at Fischers Fritz

A city of gourmet restaurants and snack bars: everything from currywurst to sushi – Berlin caters to all culinary tastes

of the many cafés. The latter – a traditional Jewish bread product with a hole in the middle – can be found in savoury form with hummus, chutney or cheese, or served sweet with jam and cream cheese.

Of course, Berlin also has plenty of haute cuisine to offer. There are currently 20 Michelin-starred restaurants in the city, at whose elegantly laid tables you can enjoy some superb (if rather pricey) cooking – often in the company of celebrities. Some star chefs also serve lunch menus,

which are a little lighter on the wallet. Either way, it's advisable to book ahead. Over the last few years, a number of young Berliners have decided to focus on dessert by opening their own ice cream parlours, cupcake bakeries or rice pudding cafés, and bringing their sweet treats to the people via selected shops, markets or food trucks. If you want to get an idea of what's on offer then pay a visit to the Markthalle Neun in Kreuzberg or the Sunday street-food market in the courtyard of the Kulturbrauerei in

Viennese coffee house with style and tradition: Café Einstein

Prenzlauer Berg. There's just one dessert that you should never order in Berlin, and that's a Berliner – as these sweet dough-nuts are actually called "Pfannkuchen" here!

CAFÉS & BREAKFAST

CAFÉ EINSTEIN ★ (151 D5) (*ØD H5*)
Traditional Viennese-style coffee house in the former villa of the silent-film star Henny Porten. The café of the same name in Mitte (Unter den Linden 42) is more modern. Both addresses have some things in common: many famous regulars, as well as a good menu (e.g. boiled beef). *Daily 8am–midnight | Tiergarten | Kurfürstenstr. 58 | tel. 030 2 63 91 90 | www.cafeeinstein.com | U1 Kurfürstenstraße*

CAFÉ LIEBLING (147 E3) (*ØD M1–2*)
Cosy café on Helmholtzplatz with news-papers and exotic warm drinks made with fresh ingredients including orange, ginger and mint tea. First-rate selection of cakes and soups at lunch. *Mon–Fri from 9am, Sat/Sun from 10am | Prenzlauer Berg | Raumerstr. 36a/corner of Dunckerstr. | tel. 030 41 19 82 09 | www.cafe-liebling.de | tram 12 Raumer Straße*

CAFÉ IM LITERATURHAUS
(139 D5) (*ØD F5*)
After a stroll down Kurfürstendamm: Coffee, cakes and freshly-made dishes in this villa with conservatory will get you going again. *Daily 9am–midnight | Charlottenburg | Fasanenstr. 23 | tel. 030 8 82 54 14 | www.literaturhaus-berlin. de | U1 Uhlandstraße*

CAFÉ SYBILLE (153 F2) (*ØD N4*)
Opened in 1953 as a milk bar in one of the GDR's monumental buildings on the street formerly known as Stalinal-lee, the charm of this place's East-Ger-man architecture has been preserved right up to the present day. A small ex-hibition depicts the history of the street, but thankfully there are no food short-ages to be found on the menu. Serves coffee, cakes and Mediterranean dishes. *Mon 11am–7pm, Tue–Sun 10am–7pm | Friedrichshain | Karl-Marx-Allee 72 | tel. 030 29 35 22 03 | www.cafe-sibylle.de | U 5 Strausberger Platz*

DACHGARTENRESTAURANT KÄFER IM DEUTSCHEN BUNDESTAG ☆ (140 A3) (*∅ J4*)

The only parliament that is daring enough to have a restaurant on its roof – and that with a fantastic view and the quality Käfer is famous for. In summer, the terrace is also open. Because of the security measures, you have to register 24 hours in advance. *Daily 9am–4:30pm and 6:30pm–midnight, breakfast 9am–noon | Mitte | Platz der Republik 1 | www.feinkost-kaefer.de | U/S Friedrichstraße*

DOUBLE EYE (159 D2) (*∅ H7*)

Galão, cappuccino or a cup of filtered coffee: there is a coffee type to suit everyone in this popular coffee shop in the Schöneberg district. *Mon–Fri 9:30am–6:30pm, Sat 10am–3:30pm | Schöneberg | Akazienstr. 22 | tel. 0179 4 56 69 60 | doubleeye.de | U 7 Eisenacher Straße*

NO FIRE NO GLORY ★ (147 E4) (*∅ M2*)

Some of the city's best baristi show off their skills here, coffee connoisseurs come for the Faema E61, rated as one of the world's best espresso machines. *Sun–Thu 9am–6pm, Fri/Sat 9am–10pm | Prenzlauer Berg | Rykestr. 45 | tel. 030 28 83 92 33 | www.nofirenoglory.de | tram M2 Marienburger Straße*

PRINCESS CHEESECAKE ☺ (152 B1) (*∅ L3*)

Magnificent cakes made with organic ingredients with an emphasis on its namesake. Cheesecake sounds ordinary, the aim here is to reach for higher goals and the results taste damn good! *Daily 10am–7pm | Mitte | Tucholskystr. 37 | tel. 030 28 09 27 60 | www.princess-cheesecake.de | S 1, 2, 25 Oranienburger Straße*

SANKT OBERHOLZ (146 C6) (*∅ L3*)

Popular café with hipsters freelancing away on their laptops while sipping their lattes. Sitting up there, guests have a fine view of one of the liveliest junctions in the city. It's quieter inside; good selection of coffees. *Mon–Thu 8am–midnight, Fri/Sat 8am–3am, Sun 9am–midnight | Mitte | Rosenthaler Str. 72a | tel.*

★ **Café Einstein**
Outstanding coffee, polite service and cosy Viennese coffee-house charm → p. 66

★ **Fischers Fritz**
Haute cuisine in the hotel's kitchen – not only for fish fans → p. 68

★ **No fire no glory**
One of the city's best espresso bars and a member of the slow-coffee movement committed to sustainable coffee cultivation → p. 67

★ **Clärchens Ballhaus**
In the most beautiful courtyard garden of the city centre you can eat meatballs or pizzas served by efficient waiters → p. 69

★ **Neni Berlin**
Creative cuisine with Mediterranean-Oriental dishes in a great atmosphere with a splendid view over the Tiergarten → p. 73

★ **Lucky Leek**
Vegan, international cuisine that is anything but joyless → p. 75

MARCO POLO HIGHLIGHTS

030 24 08 55 86 |www.sanktoberholz.de | U 8 Rosenthaler Platz

SCHWARZES CAFÉ (138 C4) *(ᗕ F5)*
For many years now this has been the place to go if you have a hankering for a continental breakfast, whatever the time of day – breakfast being served here round the clock. The atmosphere is a little faded nowadays; or in other words,

it's cosy in a Berlin sort of way. *Always open | Charlottenburg | Kantstr. 148 | tel. 030 3 13 80 38 | www.schwarzescafe-ber lin.de | S Savignyplatz*

SPREEGOLD (141 F2) *(ᗕ L3)*
A good place to escape from the hustle and bustle of Alexanderplatz for a cup of coffee or more. Good breakfasts, muffins and a changing lunch menu. *Mon–*

GOURMET RESTAURANTS

Fischers Fritz ★ (140 C4) *(ᗕ K4)*
2-star chef Christian Lohse pampers his guests in the hotel *The Regent* with slice of turbot with saffron-crustacean jus. Three-course set lunch for 47 euros, four courses in the evening for 130 euros. *Daily from 6:30am | Mitte | Charlottenstr. 49 | tel. 030 20 33 63 63 | www.fischersfritz berlin.de | U 6 Französische Straße*

Nobelhart und Schmutzig (152 B5) *(ᗕ K5)*
Billy Wagner's restaurant is "brutally local": the food comes from the surrounding region and is not served à la carte – what you get is what you eat! Everything is presented with no frills, but plenty of taste. Menu 80 euros. *Tue–Sat from 6:30pm | Kreuzberg | Friedrichstr. 218 | tel. 030 25 94 06 10 | www.nobelhart undschmutzig.com | U 6 Kochstraße*

Reinstoff (146 A6) *(ᗕ K3)*
The creative cuisine by chef Daniel Achilles in the Edison courtyards has been awarded with two Michelin stars and 18 Gault-Millau points. Garden vegetables in a St George's mushroom and rapeseed stock, crayfish on Heligoland toast or Brandenburg asparagus grown in salif-

erous clay with spruce shoot and lilac blossom vinaigrette not only impress the food critics. Menus 110–198 euros. *Tue–Sat from 7pm| Mitte | Schlegelstr. 26c | tel. 030 3 08 81 23 14 | www.reinstoff.eu | U 6 Naturkundemuseum*

Restaurant Tim Raue (152 B4) *(ᗕ K5)*
The TV and Michelin-star cook and his wife opened their restaurant in Kreuzberg in 2010. His cooking is inspired by Asia – at the highest level. Pork chin, shimeji mushrooms and king crab earned him two Michelin stars. Set meal (6 courses) 168 euros, lunch menu (3 courses) 48 euros. *Wed–Sat noon–3pm, 7pm–midnight | Kreuzberg | Rudi-Dutschke-Str. 26 | tel. 030 25 93 79 30 | www.tim-raue.com | U 6 Kochstraße*

VĀU (141 D4) *(ᗕ K4)*
The unpretentious atmosphere with Thonet chairs and modern art is perfectly suited to Kolja Kleeberg's masterfully plain menu policy. Main dishes from 40 euros, 3 lunch courses 45 euros, 6 courses in the evening 140 euros. *Mon–Sat noon–2:30pm, 7–10:30pm | Mitte | Jägerstr. 54–55 | tel. 030 20 02 97 30 | www. vau-berlin.de | U 6 Französische Straße*

Fri 7:30am–midnight, Sat/Sun 8am–midnight | Mitte | Rosa-Luxemburg-Str. 2 | tel. 030 37 58 79 80 | U /S Alexanderplatz

STRANDBAD MITTE
(141 D1) (*Ø K3*)

This place is tucked away on the shorter end of Kleine Hamburger Straße (to the south of the sports field) and boasts a large breakfast menu and an organic lunch/dinner menu. The road is pedestrianised, which makes sitting outdoors in summer even more relaxing. *Daily 9am–1am | Mitte | Kleine Hamburger Str. 16 | tel. 030 24 62 89 63 | www.strandbad-mitte. de | S 1, 2, 25 Oranienburger Straße*

GARDEN RESTAURANTS

CLÄRCHENS BALLHAUS ★
(141 D1)(*Ø K3*)

Its courtyard garden is especially attractive in summer. Organic meatballs, pizza and cakes served with a flourish – and drinks, of course! Dancing in the evening. *Daily from 11am | Mitte | Auguststr. 24 | tel. 030 282 92 95 | www.ballhaus.de | S Oranienburger Straße | Budget*

INSIDER TIP DECKSHAUS
(153 D3) (*Ø L4*)

You sit on the deck of the tug "Jeseniky" in the historical harbour and eat sprats, meatballs and fish specialities. A great place to have a beer and listen to the Spree flowing by. *Daily noon–8pm, in the summer longer if the weather permits | Mitte | Märkisches Ufer 1z | tel. 030 21 79 14 04 | www.deckshaus.de | U 2 Märkisches Museum | Budget*

FREISCHWIMMER (154 C3) (*Ø O6*)

Idyllic location on the banks of a so-called "flood channel". Creative summer cuisine. Young crowd. INSIDER TIP Canoes and kayaks can be hired! *Mon–Fri from noon,*

VÅU, a gourmet paradise near the Gendarmenmarkt

Sat/Sun from 10am | Kreuzberg | Vor dem Schlesischen Tor 2a | tel. 030 61 07 43 09 | www.freischwimmer-berlin.com | U 1 Schlesisches Tor | Budget

SCHOENBRUNN (147 F6) (*Ø N3*)

Families and the "in" crowd enjoy their sea bass or German cheese noodles in the Friedrichshain Volkspark. Perfect after (or before) a stroll through the park. Large beer garden. *Daily (in winter only Sat/Sun) from 10am | Friedrichshain | Am Schwanenteich 1 | tel. 030 453 05 65 25| www.schoenbrunn.net | tram 10 Kniprodestraße/corner of Danziger Str. | Budget– Moderate*

Chef Loriano Mura gives the finishing touches to a dish in the Bocca di Bacco

THE CLASSICS

PRATER (147 D4) (*L2*)

A cornerstone of Prenzlauer Berg, this tavern serves hearty German fare and large salads. In the beer garden, you can wash down your barbecued meats with Prater beer under the shade of the chestnut trees. *Restaurant daily from 6pm; beer garden in summer from noon | Prenzlauer Berg | Kastanienallee 7–9 | tel. 030 448 56 88 | www.pratergarten.de | U 2 Eberswalder Straße | Budget–Moderate*

TIERGARTENQUELLE (139 E1) (*G4*)

A traditional venue housed underneath the arches of the S-Bahn, and which caters to large appetites. The superb Kaiserschmarrn (an Austrian pancake dish) is big enough to feed a family. Also features draught beers from the Lemke brewery in Berlin. *Mon–Thu 4pm–midnight, Fri 4pm–1am, Sat noon–1am, Sun noon–midnight | Hansaviertel/Tiergarten | Bachstr. 6 | tel. 030 3 92 76 15 | www.tiergartenquelle.de | S 5, 7,75 Tiergarten | Budget*

WELTRESTAURANT MARKTHALLE (153 F5) (*M5*)

The right address for Sauerbraten, goulash and co. Unpretentious classics for those who still remember the student protests of '68 and their successors. In the basement: *Auster Club* with music from the 40s to the 60s. *Daily from noon | Kreuzberg | Pücklerstr. 34 | tel. 030 617 55 02 | www.weltrestaurant-markthalle.de | U 1, 15 Görlitzer Bahnhof | Budget–Moderate*

ZUR LETZTEN INSTANZ (153 D2) (*L4*)

A Berlin dinosaur. The names of the dishes such as "lawyer's breakfast" remind you that the homey pub is not far away from the law court. *Mon 5pm–1am, Tue–Sat noon–1am, Sun nooon–11pm | Mitte | Waisenstr. 14–16 | tel. 030 2 42 55 28 | www.zurletzteninstanz.de | U 2 Klosterstraße | Budget–Moderate*

RESTAURANTS: EXPENSIVE

BOCCA DI BACCO (140 C4) (*K4*)

Ravioli with loup de mer in shrimp cream, octopus carpaccio and lamb with a herb crust appeal to business people and politicians alike. Good wine list. The wine cellar, with a long wooden table for 20 guests, is especially atmospheric (more than 500 wines from Italy alone!). Reservations essential. *Mon–Sat noon–midnight, Sun 6pm–midnight | Mitte | Friedrichstr. 167–168 | tel. 030 20 67 28 28 | www.boccadi bacco.de | U 6 Französische Straße*

HORVÁTH (153 E6) (*M6*)

Not especially elegant, but the ingredients and compositions are truly splendid. The chef Sebastian Frank considers quality more important than white tablecloths. No matter whether it is slice of halibut on pumpkin purée or fillet of beef on a ragout of root vegetables in red-wine sauce, you will really savour the cuisine in this Michelin-starred restaurant. *Wed–Sun 6:30pm–11:30pm | Kreuzberg | Paul-Lincke-Ufer 44a | tel. 030 61 28 99 92 | www.res taurant-horvath.de | U 1, 8 Kottbusser Tor*

PARIS-MOSKAU (151 D2) (*H3*)

The home-style gourmet cooking – such as suckling pig and black pudding with pumpkin puree and truffle risotto – tastes particularly good in this small, half-timbered building next to the railway tracks that has managed to survive the remodelling of the government district. *Daily from 6pm; Mon–Fri also noon–3pm | Tiergarten | Alt-Moabit 141 | tel. 030 3 94 20 81 | www. paris-moskau.de | S Hauptbahnhof*

RESTAURANTS: MODERATE

ALTES ZOLLHAUS (152 C6) (*L6*)

This self-appointed "inner-city country inn" is a vision of half-timbered rural charm, complete with pike-perch from the Havel river, Brandenburg smoked eel and beetroot. In the summer, you can sit beneath chestnut trees on the terrace. *Tue–Sat from 6pm | Kreuzberg | Carl-Herz-*

Ufer 30 | tel. 030 6 92 33 00 | www.alteszollhaus-berlin.de | U 1 Prinzenstraße

BIEBERBAU (158 B4) (*G7*)

The dishes get their characteristic touch from a refined amalgamation of German cooking with a touch of the Mediterranean. Pickled knuckle of pork with truffles, pike-perch with taglierini and Maître Philippe's fine selection of cheese to finish with. Delicious. *Tue–Sat 6pm–midnight, kitchen open until 9:30pm | Wilmersdorf | Durlacher Str. 15 | tel. 030 8 53 23 90 | www.bieberbau-berlin.de | U/S Bundesplatz*

ENGELBECKEN ⊕ (148 C5) (*D5*)

Seasonal, alpine cuisine, on the lakeside at Lietzensee, homey and substantial: Weißwurst, roast pork with dumplings and red cabbage, gnocchi with sage butter for vegetarians and delicious cakes are popular. The meat comes from animals that were kept in a humane manner. *Daily; Mon–Fri from 5pm, Sat from 4pm, Sun from noon | Charlottenburg | Witzlebenstr. 31 | tel. 030 6 15 28 10 | www.engelbecken. de | U 2 Sophie-Charlotte-Platz*

ENTRECÔTE (140 C6) (*K5*)

This is the address for steak fans. French specialities from Angus beef, as well as calf's kidneys in Madeira sauce, in charming surroundings with high ceilings and friendly service. *Mon–Fri 11:30am–midnight, Sat/Sun 5:30–midnight | Mitte | Schützenstr. 5 | tel. 030 20 16 54 96 | www. entrecote.de | U 2, 6 Stadtmitte*

INSIDER TIP ▶ FRAU MITTENMANG
(147 D2) (*M1*)

Innovative German cuisine on a quiet side street, with a small menu that changes every day. For fans of goose dumplings and kale risotto. The house beer is made by a small brewery in Frankfurt an der Oder. *Daily noon–2pm and*

LOCAL SPECIALITIES

Berliner Weiße – Once a plain wheat beer, today it is served mostly with a "Schuss": choose from green (woodruff) or red (raspberry) syrup.

Buletten – Almost every butcher has these meatballs fried and ready to be eaten (photo right) and they are also sold at snack bars as curry-buletten. The word comes from the Huguenots; in French, "boulette" means little ball.

Chocolate – Those with a sweet-tooth should try some Berlin chocolate. Hamann, as well as Fassbender & Rauch, produce first rate quality – and have done so for decades.

Currywurst – Bratwurst with ketchup and curry powder (photo left) is sold on most street corners in Berlin. A snackbar owner, Herta Heuwer, came up with the recipe more than 60 years ago.

Döner Kebab – Pita bread filled with grilled veal and salad. A speciality that is just as much at home in Berlin as the currywurst.

Eisbein – Pickled knuckle of pork served with puréed peas. You will need at least one schnapps to go with it...

Kasseler – Smoked rib of pork that does not come from the town of Kassel: a Berlin butcher of the same name is responsible for its fame. A decent serving of sauerkraut to go along with it is almost obligatory.

Quark mit Leinöl – Curd cheese with linseed oil is regularly eaten in many Berlin households. The cheese is mixed with the oil and a pinch of salt and served with boiled potatoes – simple, but delicious!

Stulle – Pieces of bread with various spreads (Stullen) are once again becoming popular; sometimes old-fashioned with pork dripping, sometimes with pastrami or manchego cheese. Two slices (a sandwich) are a *Klappstulle.*

from 6pm | Prenzlauer Berg | Rodenbergstr. 37 | tel. 030 4 44 56 54 | www.fraumittenmang.de | U/S Schönhauser Allee

GOODTIME GRILL (149 D6) *(ﬆ E6)*
Good times guaranteed! Highlight: the traditional Japanese Robata grill that lends its typical smoke flavour to Asian-style fish, vegetables and meat (the best US beef fillet). *Daily noon–midnight | Charlottenburg | Kurfürstendamm 90 | tel. 030 31 99 77 70 | www.goodtime-grill. de | bus M19, M29 Lehniner Platz*

NENI BERLIN ★ (139 F4) (*G5*)
Offering an excellent view onto the Tiergarten (from the 10th floor!), the *25 hour Hotel* restaurant serves exciting dishes with Mediterranean-Oriental influences. Also caters for vegetarians. Fantastic terrace! Book a table in advance! *Mon–Fri noon–11pm, Sat/Sun 12:30–11pm | Charlottenburg | Budapester Str. 46 | tel. 030 120 22 12 00 | www.25hours-hotels.com | U 1, 2, 3 Wittenbergplatz*

NOCTI VAGUS (147 D6) (*M3*)
To test the saying "you eat with your eyes first", try visiting this darkroom restaurant with a performance programme. The most extreme experience is the surprise menu. Will you still be able to recognise chorizo, pak choi and Jerusalem artichoke when you can't see what you're eating? *Daily 10am–10pm | Prenzlauer Berg | Saarbrücker Str. 36–38 | tel. 030 74 74 91 23 | www.noctivagus.com | U 2 Senefelderplatzr*

SAGE RESTAURANT (154 A2) (*N5*)
Industrial architecture meets pizza and fresh brook char: the restaurant landscape in this gigantic brick building on the Spree varies from sophisticated cuisine to home-style cooking. Lovely lounge with a fireplace for smokers. Beach bar on the riverbank. *Tue–Sun from 2pm, in winter from 6pm | Kreuzberg | Köpenicker Str. 18–20 | tel. 030 755 49 40 71 | www.sage-restaurant.de | U1 Schlesisches Tor*

SARAH WIENER IM HAMBURGER BAHNHOF (145 E–F6) (*J3*)
Alpine cuisine (regional, seasonal and organic) is served in a side wing of the Hamburger Bahnhof Museum. Beautiful terrace on the bank of the Nordkanal. *Tue/Wed 10am–6pm, Thu 10am–8pm, Fri 10am–11pm, Sat/Sun 11am–6pm | Mitte | Invalidenstr. 50–51 | tel. 030 70 71 36 50 | www.sarahwiener.de | U/S Hauptbahnhof*

LA SOUPE POPULAIRE (147 D6) (*M3*)
Art and culinary art combined in a brewery: Star chef Tim Raue's creations are inspired by the works being exhibited, with four appetisers, four main courses, and two desserts. Cool atmosphere: a mixture between factory and restaurant. *Thu–Sat noon –2:30pm and 5:30pm–10:30pm | Prenzlauer Berg | Prenzlauer Allee 242| tel. 030 44 31 96 80 | lasoupepopulaire.de| tram M2 Prenzlauer Allee/Metzer Straße*

RESTAURANTS: BUDGET

AMPELMANN-RESTAURANT (141 D2) (*K4*)
Not only children love the restaurant's "little green traffic light man" pasta shapes and delicious pizza. Sunday brunch *(10am–2pm | 19.90 euros)*. Nice terrace on James Simon Park (banks of the Spree). *Daily 10am–10pm | Stadtbahnbogen*

The chef recommends...

*159/160 | tel. 030 84 71 07 09 | ampel
mann-restaurant.de | S Hackescher Markt*

BABA ANGORA (149 F5) *(ⓜ F5)*
First-rate Turkish cuisine with lamb dishes, grilled vegetables and seductive desserts. Homey atmosphere, reasonably-
priced set meals at lunchtime. Branch at
Goltzstr. 32 in Schöneberg. *Daily
11:30am–midnight | Charlottenburg |
Schlüterstr. 29 | tel. 030 3 23 70 96 | www.
babaangora.de | S Savignyplatz*

INSIDER TIP **BAN BAO** (147 E4) *(ⓜ M2)*
A stylish Asian burger joint serving
steamed buns layered with kimchi and

lemongrass, with sweet potato fries on
the side. The best of two culinary worlds
in one place! *Daily from noon | Pren-
zlauer Berg | Kollwitzstr. 84 | tel. 030
23 49 56 41 | www.bao-burger.de | tram
M2, 10 Prenzlauer Allee/Danziger Straße*

BERKIS Ⓥ **(159 D1)** *(ⓜ H6)*
Healthy Cretan cuisine with fresh vegetables, best olive oil and regional organic meat. Branch in the Wörtherstr. 33
(Prenzlauer Berg). *Daily 11:30am–mid-
night, Sun 1pm–midnight | Schöneberg |
Winterfeldtstr. 45 | tel. 030 77 90 04 02 |
www.berkis.de | U 1–4 Nollendorfplatz*

FISCHSCHUPPEN (155 D1) *(ⓜ P5)*
Small, relaxed bar with beautifully paint-
ed walls. Freshly prepared seafood and
fish as well as delicious fast food such as
fish'n chips (menu changes daily). Also
sells fish. *Mon–Sat 11am–10pm, Sun
noon–10pm | Friedrichshain | Boxhagen-
er Str. 68 | tel. 030 22 43 50 39 | www.
fischschuppen-berlin.de | S Ostkreuz*

GASTHAUS LENTZ (149 D5) *(ⓜ E5)*
A classic that not only attracts the old stu-
dent crowd from '68 who live in the neighbouring flats. Kölsch beer is served, there
is no music to disturb your conversation
and a variety of lunchtime specials. *Daily
from 9am | Charlottenburg | Stuttgarter
Platz 20 | tel. 030 3 24 16 19 | www.
gasthaus-lentz-berlin.de | S Charlottenburg*

NANOOSH (152 B3) *(ⓜ K4)*
This branch of an upmarket US chain specialises in Israeli cuisine. Aubergine pu-
ree, creamy hummus and tabbouleh are
on the menu, accompanied by home-
made lemonade and iced tea. *Mon–Fri
11am–11pm, Sat noon–11pm, Sun noon–
9:30pm | Mitte | Mohrenstr. 50 | tel. 030
20 14 38 70 | www.nanoosh-germany.de |
U 2, 6 Stadtmitte*

LOW BUDGET

The pizza-like slices (1.30 euros each)
with their wonderful toppings at the
Focacceria **(146 C5)** *(ⓜ L2)* *(daily from
10am | Mitte | Fehrbelliner Str. 24 | tel.
030 44 03 27 71 | U 8 Rosenthaler Platz)*
will fill you up quickly.

Japanese hot dogs? Yes: in varieties
with teriyaki sauce, wasabi mayon-
naise or shrimp, and from 4.50 euros
at *Oii Shi Hot Dogs* **(147 D3)** *(ⓜ L1)*
*(daily from noon | Prenzlauer Berg |
Schönhauser Allee 65 | tel. 030
33 85 93 94 | U/S Schönhauser Allee).*

● *Curry 36* **(160 B1)** *(ⓜ K6)* *(daily
from 9am | Kreuzberg | Mehringdamm
36 | U 6, 7 Mehringdamm)* is probably
the most popular snack bar in Kreuzberg and not only serves currywurst
(around 1.50 euros) with chips but
also pea soup (2.50 euros). You eat
standing up – and that, right through
until the early hours.

INSIDER TIP **NÖ! WEINGALERIE**
(140 C5) *(ᗰ K4)*

Small, first-class wine shop with a homey atmosphere and wine-tasting accompanied by cheese and baguette. *Mon–Fri noon–1am | Mitte | Glinkastr. 23 | tel. 030 2 01 08 71 | www.cafe-noe.de | U2, 6 Stadtmitte*

ROSA LISBERT (150 B1) *(ᗰ G3)*

An expanded street-food stand inside the renovated Arminius market hall that serves French specialities. The crispy tartes flambées here come with the traditional topping of bacon and onions, as well as more unusual combinations such as eel, sauerkraut and cured horsemeat. *Tue–Sat noon–10pm | Moabit | Arminiusstr. 2–4 | tel. 0152 21 98 29 23 | www.rosalisbert.de | U 9 Turmstraße*

VEGAN

GOODIES (154 C1) *(ᗰ O4)*

This café offers cream cake without cream and milk-free white coffee, accompanied by bagels, wraps and smoothies – no animal was harmed during their production. *Mon–Fri 7am–8pm, Sat/Sun 9am–8pm | Friedrichshain| Warschauer Str. 69 | tel. 030 89 65 49 73 | www.goodies-berlin. de | U 5 Frankfurter Tor | Budget*

KOPPS (146 B6) *(ᗰ K3)*

This trendy vegan venue proves that veganism doesn't have to be a joyless affair. A five-course menu with wine costs 79 euros, though the INSIDER TIP Sunday brunch is much cheaper (13.50 euros). *Mon–Fri from 6pm, Sat/Sun from 9:30am | Mitte | Linienstr. 94 | tel. 030 43 20 97 75 | U 8 Rosenthaler Platz| Expensive*

LUCKY LEEK ★ (147 D5) *(ᗰ L2)*

Refined cuisine with changing, seasonal menus, served on sleek wooden tables.

Good and reasonably-priced: La Focacceria in Mitte

Some creations are so exquisite that it almost seems a shame to eat them. Make sure you leave room for dessert! *Wed–Sun 6pm–10pm | Prenzlauer Berg | Kollwitzstr. 54 | tel. 030 66 40 87 10 | www.luckyleek.com | U 2 Senefelderplatz | Moderate*

THE BOWL (154 B1) *(ᗰ O5)*

"Clean eating": *The Bowl* is entirely dedicated to this diet, which avoids industrially produced food – so as well as animal products, you won't find any sugar or gluten on the menu either. The result is anything but joyless! Located on the first floor above the vegan supermarket *Veganz* (see p. 79). *Tue–Sun 10am–11:30pm, Mon noon–11:30pm | Friedrichshain | Warschauer Str. 33 | U/S Warschauer Straße | Budget*

SHOPPING

WHERE TO START?

Alexa on Alexanderplatz (Mitte) and **Tauentzienstraße** near the Gedächtniskirche (Charlottenburg) will be the first choice for fans of today's fast-selling fashion labels. The latter is also the home of the **KaDeWe** (Department Store of the West), that is steeped in tradition. Those who are more interested in small boutiques with clothes by Berlin designers will find what they are looking for in the **Hackesche Höfe** and on **Alte** and **Neue Schönhauser Straße** (Mitte). **Bergmannstraße** (Kreuzberg) is the place for second-hand articles.

Berlin has so many shopping streets that it is impossible to list them all. And, if you are looking for the real shopping heart of the city, you won't be able to pin-point it. There is a simple reason for this: there are shopping areas in almost every district.

In Mitte, this is Friedrichstraße with its exclusive boutiques. The clientele in the *Galeries Lafayette* and *Quartier 206* is just as international as the brand names. On the other hand, Germany's largest Kaufhof department store and the *Alexa shopping centre* attract shoppers to Alexanderplatz, while on Leipziger Platz, the *Mall of Berlin* is waiting for customers. Kurfürstendamm, with its many designer boutiques, and Tauentzienstraße with *Peek & Cloppenburg* and *KaDeWe* depart-

Shopping areas and arcades are not just concentrated on the centre – each district has its own shopping centres and specialist shops

ment stores and the Europacenter are the pride and joy of Charlottenburg's retail world. On Budapester Straße you'll find the chic *Bikini Berlin* complex with its designer boutiques and pop-up stores. In Zehlendorf and Steglitz people stroll along Schlossstraße. And, then there are all the resourceful shop-owners in smaller streets such as Kastanienallee in Prenzlauer Berg (also called "Castingallee" because of its fashion boutiques) or Wühlischstraße in Friedrichshain with fashion, shoes and

bags by Berlin designers. The area around the Hackesche Höfe is also renowned for its fashion boutiques.

ANTIQUE & SECOND-HAND

ANTIK- UND BUCHMARKT
(152 B2) (*ﾉ K3–4*)
The banks of the Spree by Museum Island offer a majestic backdrop for a weekend stroll – and you might even find a hidden treasure buried among the old vinyl records, household goods, postcards and

Sweet delicacies from Istanbul in the Confiserie Orientale

coins. *Sat/Sun 11am–5pm | Mitte | Am Kupfergraben | www.antik-buchmarkt. de | U/S Friedrichstraße*

DÜWAL (138 B4) (*D F5*)

Lovers of old books treasure those on offer at this renowned shop. The valuable tomes are stacked to the ceiling. *Mo–Fri 3pm–6pm, Sat 11am–2pm | Charlottenburg | Schlüterstr. 17 | www. duewal.de | S Savignyplatz*

 **INSIDER TIP** ▶ PLATTEN PEDRO
(149 D2) (*D D–E3*)

Berlin's largest source of old records with, among other things around 200,000 singles. The demanding collector will find everything from folk music to hard rock to make his heart beat faster. *Mon–Fri 10am–6pm, in winter until 4:50pm, Sat 10am–2:30pm | Charlottenburg | Tegeler Weg 102 | www.platten-pedro.de | U 7 Mierendorffplatz*

BEAUTY

NIVEA HOUSE (140 C4) (*D K4*)

Enormous selection of cosmetics. You can have a quick restoration session in the beauty salon. A facial (25 minutes) costs 25 euros. If you are tense, a neck-and-shoulder massage will loosen you up. *Mon–Sat 10am–8pm | Mitte | Unter den Linden 28 | tel. 030 20 45 61 60 | www. nivea.de | U/S Brandenburger Tor*

THE ENGLISH SCENT
(138 B3) (*D E–F5*)

Classy shop with limited opening times famous for its somewhat eccentric British perfumes that cannot be found in any other shops in Berlin. Most of the scents come from purveyors by appointment to Her Majesty the Queen. You will receive expert advice if you are not sure which perfume suits you best. *Tue, Thu, Fri 10am–2pm, Sat 10am–3pm | Charlottenburg | Goethestr. 15 | www. english-scent.de | S Savignyplatz*

DELICATESSEN

INSIDER TIP CONFISERIE ORIENTALE
(140 C1) (*ω K3*)
One of Istanbul's best confectioners produces exclusively for this small shop: marzipan and nougat sweets and all sorts of exotic flavours. Try some yourself over a cup of mocha in the shop and then take some home with you packed up beautifully in little boxes. *Mon–Fri 11am–7pm, Sat/Sun 11am–6pm | Mitte | Linienstr. 113 | www.confiserie-orientale-berlin.com | S 1, 2, 25 Oranienburger Straße*

FRANZ KARL ★ (147 F5) (*ω N2*)
The best cakes and gateaux far and wide make this confectionery by Franz-Karl Kaufmann a paradise for all fans of Austrian patisserie: whether New York cheesecake, Sachertorte, or Gugelhupf: The creations by this ex-head patissier of an international hotel chain are all delicious. *Wed–Sun noon–6:30pm | Prenzlauer Berg | Bötzowstr. 15 | www. kuchenkultur-franz-karl.de | tram M10 Bötzowstraße*

GOLDHAHN & SAMPSON
(147 E3) (*ω M1*)
Taking a look at all of the spices here is like a journey around the world. Cooking courses are held in the rear section of the shop. A limited – but first-rate – selection of wines and spirits. *Mon–Fri 8am–8pm, Sat 9am–8pm | Prenzlauer Berg | Dunckerstr. 9 | www.goldhahnund sampson.de | U 2 Eberswalder Straße*

VEGANZ ⊙ (146 C2) (*ω O*)
From cottage cheese to dog food – in Europe's first vegan supermarket, everything is strictly vegan and mostly organic. On Sundays brunch *(10am–4pm | 14.90 euros)*. Cooking classes. Branches in Friedrichshain *(Warschauer Str. 33)* and Kreuzberg *(Marheinekeplatz 15)*. *Mon–Sat 8am–9pm | Prenzlauer Berg | Schivelbeiner Str. 34 | tel. 030 44 03 60 48 | www.veganz.de | U-/S Schönhauser Allee*

⭐ **Flea market am 17. Juni**
The classic among Berlin's flea markets → p. 81

⭐ **KaDeWe**
Even just visiting the gourmet floor is a great experience → p. 82

⭐ **Quartier 206**
Sophisticated atmosphere, fine selection, no hurry – welcome to this designer departement store → p. 83

⭐ **14 oz.**
Not only VIPs like shopping here as if they were in a private living room → p. 83

⭐ **Trippen**
Wood and leather designer shoes of cult status; the cool showroom looks like a gallery → p. 84

⭐ **Franz Karl**
One of the city's best confectioneries with the finest Austrian patisseries and long queues at the counter → p. 79

⭐ **Markt am Maybachufer**
Large Turkish families buy vegetables by the crate, the merchants try to outshout each other → p. 85

MARCO POLO HIGHLIGHTS

FLEA MARKETS

THIS & THAT

AUS BERLIN (141 F2) *(ĴĴ L3)*
Products from more than 200 Berlin designers and producers add colour to the drab prefabricated concrete building. These range from painted storm jackets to heartbreak pills. You can even find Gorbachev Vodka, which is produced in Berlin-Reinickendorf. Sometimes, DJs work the turntables. *Mon–Sat 10am–8pm | Mitte | Karl-Liebknecht-Str. 9 | www.ausberlin.de | U/S Alexanderplatz*

INSIDERTIP **ERFINDERLADEN**
(147 D4) *(ĴĴ L2)*
For everyone who has always wanted to own a necktie tying aid or a device for growing avocado plants. This place sells brand-new products that haven't yet reached the mass market. *Mon–Sat 11am–8pm | Prenzlauer Berg | Lychener Str. 8 | www.erfinderladen-berlin.de | U 2 Eberswalder Straße*

INTERSHOP 2000 (154 C2) *(ĴĴ O5)*
You will find (almost) everything that was part of everyday life in former East Germany in this erstwhile Konsum shop: Mitropa chinaware, eggcups and Free German Youth (FDJ) pennants. Ideal for rummaging around in the past era of Socialist design. *Wed–Fri 2–6pm, Sat/Sun noon–6pm | Friedrichshain | Danneckerstr. 8 | www.intershop.2000.com | U/S Warschauer Straße*

KPM (139 D–E 1–2) *(ĴĴ F4)*
Elegant items from the Royal Porcelain Factory (KPM) are not only sold in the magnificently restored old buildings but also displayed in a fascinating way – with demonstration workshops, guided tours, special exhibitions and a café. In additional room on the other side of the courtyard you can purchase the some-

what cheaper B-goods. *Mon–Sat 10am–6pm | admission KPM Welt 10 euros | Tiergarten | Wegelystr. 1 | www.kpm-berlin.de | S 7, 9, 75 Tiergarten*

MODULOR (153 D5) *(ĴĴ L5)*
With over 7,000 items of decoration and model making items, this store is not only popular with DIY enthusiasts and architects. The place to go for corrugated cardboard, perforated sheets, film or paper – also available in its online shop. With sewing studio and consultation service. *Mon–Fri 9am–8pm, Sat 10am–6pm | Kreuzberg | Prinzenstr. 85 | www.modulor.de | U 8 Moritzplatz*

INSIDERTIP **ORIGINAL UNVERPACKT** ☺
(153 F6) *(ĴĴ M6)*
Make sure you bring some Tupperware with you when you shop for groceries here, as the goods at this supermarket all come without packaging. Whether you're buying pasta, nuts or toothpaste, you'll need to bring your own containers – all for the good of the environment. *Mon–Sat 9:30am–8pm | Kreuzberg | Wiener Straße 16 | www.original-unverpackt.de | U 1 Görlitzer Bahnhof*

FLEA MARKETS

AM MAUERPARK ●
(146 C3–4) *(ĴĴ L1–2)*
A key fixture for any Sunday in Berlin. Go for a stroll among old spoons, antique furniture and screen-printed bags produced by young designers before stopping for a Turkish vegetable flatbread, washed down with fresh orange juice. After that, head to the park, where after 3pm you'll find mass karaoke sessions and a different musician playing by every tree. *Sun 9am–6pm | Prenzlauer Berg | Eberswalder Str. | www.flohmarktimmauerpark.de | U 2 Eberswalder Straße*

BOXHAGENER PLATZ (154 C1) (*∅ O5*)
A small square in the eastern part of Friedrichshain with a cosy flea market, where among private vendors, professionals also sell their stuff. The nearby clothing, jewellery, and record and CD dealers sometimes demand excessive prices. But here bartering is the order of the day. The second-hand dealers are in the upper section towards the Siegessäule

Berlin's flea markets offer all kinds of useful and unusual second-hand articles

cafés are ideal places to sit and watch the dealers and bargain-hunters. *Sun 10am–6pm | Friedrichshain | Boxhagener Platz | U5 Samariterstraße*

NOWKOELLN (153 E–F6) (*∅ M6*)
The "in" flea market on Maybachufer with chic T-shirts by Berlin designers, retro second-hand stuff and other knick-knacks the hip people who live here need in their lofts. Live music and grilled sausages. *April–Nov 1st and 3rd Sun in the month 10am–6pm | Neukölln | Maybachufer | www.nowkoelln.de | U8 Schönleinstraße*

FLEA MARKET AM 17. JUNI ⭐
(150 A–B 3–4) (*∅ F–G4*)
The most famous flea market in the west of the city. The many professional antique, and the arts and crafts people in the other direction near Ernst-Reuter-Platz. *Sat/Sun 10am–5pm | Charlottenburg | Straße des 17. Juni | www.berlinertroedel markt.com | S Tiergarten*

DEPARTMENT STORES

BIKINI BERLIN ● (139 E4) (*∅ G5*)
In the factory-style shopping centre opposite the Gedächtniskirche, you can find creative accessories by Berlin designers, but also fashion by Berlin label Blutsgeschwister or outdoor outfitter Noth Face. Splendid roof terrace with view onto the monkeys in the zoo. *Mon–Sat 10am–8pm | Charlottenburg | Budapester Str. 38–50 | www.bikiniberlin. de | U/S Zoologischer Garten*

FASHION

DUSSMANN ● (140 C3) (*K4*)
This "cultural department store" boasts four floors of CDs, DVDs, videos, books, games and software. The many special offers will whet your appetite. Big non-German book section. And you can have

KADEWE ★ (139 F5) (*G5*)
It is worth visiting the KaDeWe just to go to the delicatessen department on the 6th floor: they have (almost) everything from artichokes to zabaglione. The selection of high-fashion labels on the clothing floors

Even those who don't buy anything cannot help but admire the domed round building of the Galeries Lafayette

a coffee and cake under the INSIDER TIP hanging garden with 6,000 tropical plants by Patric Blanc. *Mon–Fri 9am–midnight, Sat 9am–11:30pm | Mitte | Friedrichstr. 90 | www.kulturkaufhausde | U/S Friedrichstraße*

GALERIES LAFAYETTE (140 C4) (*K4*)
An eldorado for shoppers with a wonderful delicatessen department, international fashion and sensational architecture. *Mon–Sat 10am–8pm | Mitte | Friedrichstr. 76–78 | U 6 Französische Straße*

is also overwhelming. *Mon–Thu 10am–8pm, Fri 10am–9pm, Sat 9:30–8pm | Schöneberg | Tauentzienstr. 21–24 | U 1, 2, 3 Wittenbergplatz*

FASHION

FETTEBEUTE (154 C1) (*O5*)
A stylish shop selling – quite literally – a colourful mixture of goods. You can find affordable clothes made by local fashion designers in amongst better-known labels like Mavi and Desigual. *Mon–Sat noon–8pm | Friedrichshain | Koperni-*

kusstr. 22 | www.fettebeute-shop.de | tram M13 Libauer Straße

KAUF DICH GLÜCKLICH
(146 C5) (*Ω L2*)

Independent labels, mainly from Berlin and Scandinavia, as well as accessories such as shoes and bags – plus an in-store café selling fresh waffles. *Daily 10am–8pm | Prenzlauer Berg | Kastanienallee 54 | www.kaufdichgluecklich-shop. de | tram M1, 12 Zionskirchplatz*

NIX ☻ (141 D2) (*Ω K3*)

Discrete colours, robust materials and simple cuts are the secrets of Barbara Gebhardt's success. A Nix coat or skirt is just as suited for everyday wear as it is for visiting the opera. *Mon–Sat 11am–7pm | Mitte | Oranienburger Str. 32 | www.nix.de | S1, 2, 25 Oranienburger Straße*

QUARTIER 206 ★ (140 C5) (*Ω K4*)

Elegant designer shop with fashion by Cerruti, Yves Saint-Laurent, Strenesse, Gucci and others. Bargains in the "Department-Store". *Mon–Fri 11am–8pm, Sat 10am–6pm | Mitte | Friedrichstr. 71 | www. quartier206.com | U 6 Französische Straße*

SUPERMARCHÉ ☻ (153 F6) (*Ω M6*)

Sustainably produced and inexpensive T-shirts, jeans and dresses. The store invites you to delve into fair trade fashion. Shop with a good conscience and without the alternative touch. *Mon–Fri 11am–7pm, Sat 11am–6pm | Kreuzberg | Wiener Str. 16 | www.supermarche-berlin.de | U 1 Görlitzer Bahnhof*

UNIQLO (158 B5) (*Ω G5*)

The first German branch of the Japanese answer to H&M and Zara. The name is an amalgam of "unique" and "clothing", and the brand stands for classic style and low prices. The fashion from Hello Kitty's homeland ranges from quilted gilets and smart blouses to quirky T-shirts with comic-book prints. There is now also a second branch in the *Mall of Berlin (Leipziger Platz 16)*. *Mon–Thu 10am–8:30pm, Fri/Sat 10am–9pm | Charlottenburg | Tauentzienstr. 7 b/c | www.uniqlo.com | U 1, 2 Wittenbergplatz*

WERTVOLL ☻ (147 E5) (*Ω M2*)

Organic cotton, recycled materials and pine fibres are the basic ingredients for underwear, blouses and dresses. Labels such as People Tree, Do You Green and format guarantee fair production conditions and part of the profits are donated to charitable organisations. *Mon–Fri 10am–8pm, Sat 10am–6pm | Prenzlauer Berg | Marienburger Str. 39 | www.wertvoll-berlin.com | tram M 2 Marienburger Straße*

14 OZ. ★ ☻ (141 E2) (*Ω L3*)

Mixture of fashionable brands and eco-streetwear. The shop is run by Karl-Heinz Müller, the initiator of the „Bread & Butter" fashion fair. You can make your purchases in the private atmosphere of a living room in some rooms on the first floor set up especially for this purpose. Branch at *Kurfürstendamm 194*, outlet store 500 m (1,640 ft) further on at *Memhardtstr. 7* near Alexanderplatz. *Mon–Sat 11am–8pm | Mitte | Neue Schönhauser Str. 13 | www.14oz. net | U 8 Weinmeisterstraße*

SHOES

INSIDER TIP JÜNEMANNS
PANTOFFEL-ECK (147 D6) (*Ω L3*)

Felt slippers like grandma used to wear are stacked to the ceiling of this small work-room-cum-shop. The products of the more than 100-year-old family business have developed a cult status of their own. *Mon–Fri 9am–6pm | Mitte | Torstr. 39 | www. pantoffeleck.de | U2 Rosa-Luxemburg-Platz*

Trippen in the Hackesche Höfe displays its shoes as if they were works of art

LUCCICO (141 E1) (*M L3*)
Unusual design, fine workmanship and good value for money – all this leads to the house in the "shopping Bermuda triangle" being full all the time. Other branches at Oranienburger Str. 23 (outlet) and Bergmannstr. 8 (Kreuzberg). *Mon–Fri noon–8pm, Sat 11am–8pm | Mitte | Weinmeisterstr. 12 | www.luccico.de | U 8 Weinmeisterstraße*

TRIPPEN ★ ⊕ (141 E2) (*M L3*)
Absolutely first-rate, designer wood and leather shoes that have created a furore throughout the world. The showroom with the models displayed under spotlights in individual niches is more reminiscent of a gallery than a shop. The company's motto is "ecologically honest and anatomically sensible". *Mon–Fri 11am–8pm, Sat 10am–8pm | Mitte | Rosenthaler Str. 40/41 | Hackesche Höfe IV & VI | www.trippen.com | S Hackescher Markt*

ZEHA (147 E4) (*M M2*)
Berlin label with cult status with classic shoes made of calf leather and sneakers and court shoes of the highest quality. There are branches in Schöneberg *(Belziger Str. 21)* and Kreuzberg *(Friesenstr. 7). Mon–Fri noon–8pm, Sat 10am–6pm | Prenzlauer Berg | Prenzlauer Allee 213 | www.zeha-berlin.de | tram M2 Marienburger Straße*

SECOND HAND

COLOURS BERLIN (160 B2) (*M K7*)
Tucked away in an inner courtyard building, experimental fashionistas have tons of second-hand clothes to choose from on one vast floor. Clothes are assorted into styles and colours. 30% discount on all clothes on Tuesdays between 11am and 3pm. *Mon–Sat 11am–7pm | Kreuzberg | Bergmannstr. 102 | www.kleidermarkt.de | U 6, 7 Mehringdamm*

GARMENTS VINTAGE (143 D3) (*M L–M1*)
Pick up your own piece of cinema history: a large proportion of the scarcely-worn designer clothes here were originally used during film and TV productions. The two owners are costume designers, which is how they get hold of their goods. A second branch can be found

at Linienstr. 204. *Mon–Sat noon–7pm | Prenzlauer Berg | Stargarder Str. 12a | www.garments-vintage.de | U/S Schönhauser Allee*

MADONNA (138 A5) (*∅ E5*)

Second-hand designer and brand names. Versace coats, Jil Sander pullovers and Chanel costumes look like new. Bad buys on the part of their first owners? There is a branch for men at Mommsenstr. 43. *Mon–Fri noon–7pm, Sat noon–4pm | Charlottenburg | Mommsenstr. 57 | www.madonna-adon.de | S Charlottenburg*

WEEKLY MARKETS

INSIDERTIP KARL-AUGUST–PLATZ ♨
(149 E4–5) (*∅ E5*)

Specialities from all over Europe make this market a real delicatessen paradise. Cheese from the Alps and organic carrots, fresh noodles, jam, high-quality fruit and much more not only attract gourmets from Charlottenburg. *Wed 7am–1:30pm, Sat 7am–2:30pm | Charlottenburg | Karl-August-Platz | U 7 Wilmersdorfer Straße*

KOLLWITZMARKT ♨
(147 D4–5) (*∅ M2*)

Many food-conscious local residents buy here: organic vegetables and meat and delicatessen from regional producers. Thu: organic food only; Sat: a wider selection. *Thu noon–7pm, Sat 9am–4pm | Prenzlauer Berg | Kollwitzplatz | U2 Senefelderplatz*

MARKT AM MAYBACHUFER ★ ♨
(153 E–F6) (*∅ M6*)

Everything the large Anatolian family needs can be bought at the "Turkish market". Grapes, tomatoes and aubergines are sold by the crate. The young German smart set from Kreuzberg are more attracted to antipasti and organic

cheese. Berliners call this a "Kreuzberg melange". *Tue, Fri 11am–6:30pm | Neukölln | Maybachufer | U 8 Schönleinstraße*

WINTERFELDTMARKT (159 D1) (*∅ H6*)

Visiting this weekly market is an absolute must in the Schöneberg gay and academic scene. And afterwards just watch the world go by from one of the cafés. *Wed 8am–2pm, Sat 8am–4pm | Schöneberg | Winterfeldtplatz | 1, 2 Nollendorfplatz*

LOW BUDGET

Berlin's largest Asia market, the *Dong Xuang Center* **(165 E3)** (*∅ Q3*) (*Wed–Mon 10am–8pm | Lichtenberg | Herzbergstr. 128–139 | dongxuan-berlin.de | tram 21, M4, M5, M8 Herzbergstraße/Industriegebiet*), offers cheap groceries, clothing, electronics, household goods and rrestaurants in six halls.

The *Marc-O'Polo-Outlet* **(148 C4)** (*∅ D4*) (*Mon–Fri 10am–7pm, Sat 10am–6pm | Charlottenburg | Kaiserdamm 7 | U 2 Sophie-Charlotte-Platz*) is a haven for bargain hunters.

Discounts of up to 70 percent on high-street fashion brands at the *Zalando Outlet* **(154 A2)** (*∅ N5*) (*Mon–Sat 10am–8pm | Kreuzberg | Köpenicker Str. 20 | www.zalando-outlet.de/berlin | U 1 Schlesisches Tor*).

New and used CDs and records are offered at *Logo Records* **(160 B2)** (*∅ K7*) (*Mon–Fri noon–7pm, Sat 11am–5pm | Kreuzberg | Nostitzstr. 32 10 | U7 Gneisenaustraße*).

ENTERTAINMENT

WHERE TO START?
If you want to have a good time and not spend much money, the Neukölln district around **Weserstraße** is the place to go *(U7, 8 Hermannstraße)*. You will find many popular bars and clubs (including Riva Bar and House of Weekend Club) in Mitte between **Alexanderplatz** and **Hackescher Markt** or around the **Oberbaumbrücke** that connects Kreuzberg and Friedrichshain. At Watergate, you can dance with a view of the Spree. Nearby at the Ostbahnhof, the queues in front of Berghain show you that this is one of the most popular clubs in the world.

You'll miss the best of Berlin if you spend your nights in bed. One of the world's most famous party scenes only gets going after midnight and doesn't get home before lunch the following day!

Over 300 clubs play everything from electronic music to indie rock, as well as venues where you can test out your swing dancing or waltzing skills. Countless bars and pubs sell craft beer and cocktails, though among the younger crowd the trend is to buy bottles or cans from an off-licence to save money during the summer. The neighbours don't always approve of this practice, however, and for years the authorities have searched for solutions to meet Berlin's nightlife needs while ensuring residents can get a good night's sleep. Sometimes the clubs close

Photo: Club Watergate at Oberbaumbrücke

First stop, a theatre performance and then on to a bar and later dancing until dawn

down, sometimes the locals move to quieter neighbourhoods. Culture vultures are well-provided for by over 50 theatres and 300 cinemas – despite its financial issues, the city doesn't stint when it comes to the arts. Berlin has three opera houses – more than any other city in the world!

BARS

BECKETTS KOPF (147 D3) *(ψ M1)*
Don't be put off by the locked door! If you ring the bell then you can be sure of some excellent drinks – though with unusual names, such as "Mother in Law". *Daily from 8pm | Prenzlauer Berg | Pappelallee 64 | tel. 030 44 03 58 80 | www. becketts-kopf.de | tram 12 Raumerstraße*

CORDOBAR (152 C1) *(ψ K3)*
An oenological institution serving superb wines, and run by a former sommelier at the Hotel Adlon and a record-label boss. Also has a snack menu that changes every month. *Tue–Sat 6pm–2am | Mitte | Große Hamburger Str. 32 |*

You can chill or dance the evening away at the Strandbar Mitte

tel. 030 27 58 12 15 | www.cordobar.net | S 5, 7, 75 Hackescher Markt

KEYSER SOZE
(152 B1) (*🕮 K3*)
Sit down at one of the rickety wooden tables in this place and enjoy some good cocktails, as well as breakfast or traditional German fare. The name is taken from the mysterious mob boss in Bryan Singer's film "The Usual Suspects". *Daily from 7:30am | Mitte | Tucholskystr. 33 | tel. 030 28 59 94 89 | www.keyser-soze.de | S 1, 2, 25 Oranienburger Straße*

KLUNKERKRANICH ★
(161 F3) (*🕮 M–N7*)
An alternative bar with great views, located on the roof of the Neukölln Arcaden shopping centre. Sit down on the wooden boards between the herb garden and the timber bar and enjoy cocktails, beer or coffee. Breakfast and pasta are also available for the peckish. Access via the car park. *In the summer Mon–Sat from 10am, Sun from noon, spring and autumn Thu/Fri from 4pm, Sat/Sun from noon, closed during the winter | Neukölln | Karl-Marx-Str. 66 | www.klunkerkranich.de | U 7 Rathaus Neukölln*

MONKEY BAR
(139 F4) (*🕮 G5*)
Excellent view of the monkeys in the zoo, best drinks and friendly guests. This mixture is attracting Berliners back to the city's west with the shopping centre Bikini Berlin and the *25hours Hotel* where this bar is located. *Sun–Thu noon–1am, Fri/Sat noon–2am | Charlottenburg | Budapester Str. 40/10th floor | www.25hours-hotels.com | U 1, 2, 3 Wittenbergplatz*

NEWTON (140 C5) (*🕮 K4*)
The nude photographs by the late Helmut Newton might distract you from your oysters, champagne and well-mixed cocktails. There is a cigar lounge on the first floor for those so inclined. *Sun–Thu 10am–3am, Fri/Sat 10am–4am | Mitte | Charlottenstr. 57 | tel. 030 20 29 54 21 | www.newton-bar.de | U 6 Französische Straße*

RIVA (141 E2) *(Ⓜ L3)*
Guests sit at the oval bar under a railway arch; the bottle rack in the centre is modelled on the *Titanic*. This is the place for aesthetes with a fondness for cultivated cocktails. *Tue–Sat from 6pm | Mitte | Dircksenstr. 142 | tel. 030 24 72 26 88 | www.riva-berlin.de |S Hackescher Markt*

SOLAR (152 A5) *(Ⓜ J5)*
Sip your cocktails on the 16th floor with a great view. Especially after the trip in a glass lift up the façade of the building has given you your first thrill! By the way, you can also enjoy a Mediterranean meal here. *Sun–Thu 6pm–2am, Fri/Sat until 4am | Kreuzberg | Stresemannstr. 76 | tel. 0163 765 27 00 | www.solarberlin.com | S1, 25 Anhalter Bahnhof*

STRANDBAR MITTE
(141 D2) *(Ⓜ K3)*
Young and old meet on the banks of the Spree in summer to order their cocktails, coffee or beer from the self-service bar and relax in the deckchairs with a view towards the Museumsinsel. Dancing from 8pm. *May–Sept daily from 10am | Mitte | Monbijoustr. 3 | www.strandbar-mitte.de | S1, 25 Oranienburger Straße*

WEINBAR RUTZ ★ (140 B–C1) *(Ⓜ K3)*
1,001 different wines lie waiting for you in the racks of this carefully-styled bar. The wine list is enormous but a sommelier will help you make your choice: in addition, exquisite cooking. *Tue–Sat from 4pm, meals from 6:30pm | Mitte | Chausseestr. 8 | tel. 030 24 62 87 60 | www.rutz-weinbar.de | U6 Oranienburger Tor*

BREWERIES

HAUSBRAUEREI ESCHENBRÄU
(145 D4) *(Ⓜ H1)*
On the inside, a rustic tavern; on the outside, an inviting beer garden. The beer is freshly brewed, but unfiltered, so it's served unusually cloudy. *Daily from 3pm, in the winter from 5pm | Wedding | Triftstr. 67 | tel. 0162 4 93 19 15 | www.eschenbraeu.de | U 6, 9 Leopoldplatz*

MARCO POLO HIGHLIGHTS

★ Weinbar Rutz
Best wine bar in Berlin with over 1000 wines and gourmet cuisine → p. 89

★ Klunkerkranich
Alternative rooftop bar with amazing views in trendy Neukölln → p. 88

★ Berghain/Panoramabar
Internationally popular bar in a disused heating plant → p. 90

★ Lido
The place to be for indie pop fans → p. 91

★ Bar jeder Vernunft
Shows, variety performances and top cuisine in the mirror tent → p. 92

★ Friedrichstadt-Palast
Glitz and glamour: the world's largest show stage with fabulous dancers → p. 94

★ Philharmonie
A must for classic fans: magnificent acoustics and top orchestras → p. 95

★ Deutsches Theater
As in its best days: top-quality classics → p. 97

PFEFFERBRÄU (147 D5) (*ill L2*)

Over the last few years, beer has once again started to be brewed on the former site of the Pfefferberg brewery, which closed after the Second World War. Visit the stylish tap room to sample the strong Pilsner or unfiltered malt beer. *Tue–Sun from 5:30pm | Prenzlauer Berg | Schönhauser Allee 176 | tel. 030 4 73 77 36 40 | www.pfefferbraeu.de | U 2 Senefelderplatz*

INSIDERTIP▶ PRIVATBRAUEREI AM ROLLBERG (154 A6) (*ill M7*)

The tavern here is separated from the brew kettle by just a sheet of glass. This large site was formerly used as a brewery by Berliner Kindl; now, the small private brewery shares the space with a centre for contemporary art. *Thu 5pm–11pm, Fri/Sat 5pm–midnight | Neukölln | Am Sudhaus 3 | tel. 030 68 08 45 77 | www. rollberger.de | U 8 Boddinstraße*

CLUBS

BERGHAIN/PANORAMABAR ★
(154 B1) (*ill N5*)

Techno-electro club next to the Ostbahnhof that has fans from all over the world. Anyone lucky enough to get past the bouncers can party non-stop under the 18 m/60 ft-high ceilings of this former power station for up to three days and nights. All this with art on the walls and a laid-back atmosphere. *Fri/Sat from midnight | admission 12–16 euros | Friedrichshain | Am Wriezener Bahnhof | S Ostbahnhof*

INSIDERTIP▶ CZAR HAGESTOLZ
(165 E3) (*ill R–S4*)

If you're a fan of the old-school Berlin club culture that spontaneously burst into life in the city's empty factories during the 1990s, then you will love *Czar Hagestolz,* which offers DIY charm on the loading ramp of a former stockyard. The playlist focuses on electronic music. *Fri/Sat from 1am | admission 10 euros | Marzahn | Marzahner Chaussee 51 | tel. 030 69 56 68 40 | www.czar-hagestolz.de | S 5, 7, 75 Friedrichsfelde-Ost*

GRETCHEN (152 B6) (*ill J6*)

Set on two floors in the former stables of a Prussian regiment, this club attracts a mixed crowd of all ages. Music from electro to dubstep, indie to jazz. Also theatre and workshops. *Fri/Sat from 11:30pm, otherwise depending on the event | Kreuzberg | Obentrautstr. 19–21 | tel. 030 25 92 27 02 | www.gretchen-club. de | U 6, 7 Mehringdamm*

LOW BUDGET

The free concerts of the students from the *Hanns Eisler Music College* at *Charlottenstr. 55* (140 C5) (*ill K4*) (*U 2, 6 Stadtmitte*) and *Schlossplatz 7* (141 E4) (*ill L4*) (*U 2 Hausvogteiplatz*) locations present the virtuosos of the future. *Tickets: tel. 030 2 03 09 21 01 | www.hfm-berlin.de*

The ● *Sageclub* (153 D3–4) (*ill M5*) (*Kreuzberg | Köpenicker Str. 76 | www. sage-club.de | U 8 Heinrich-Heine-Straße*) presents "Rock at Sage" on Thu – admission is free from 8 to 10 pm.

The *frannz-Club* (147 D4) (*ill L2*) (*Prenzlauer Berg | Schönhauser Allee 36 | www.frannz.de | U 2 Eberswalder Straße*) presents pop/rock and eighties on Sat. Before midnight, admission is free with a password found on their website!

GRIESSMÜHLE (154 C6) *(∅ O8)*
An old pasta factory with an outdoor area by the Neukölln Ship Canal. The door policy is as moderate as the entry fee, and the weekend party runs from Friday evening until Sunday night with techno, house and electro. *Fri 10pm–Sun midnight | from 5 euros | Neukölln | Sonnenallee 221 | tel. 030 20 63 96 50 | www. griessmuehle.de | S 41, 42 Sonnenallee*

HOUSE OF WEEKEND
(141 F2) *(∅ L–M3)*
Dancing to electronic music on the 15th floor of the former "Haus des Reisens" East German travel organisation high up above Alexanderplatz. The ☀ terrace and bar are only open in summer – the view is magnificent. *Daily from 11pm | admission 10–15 euros | Mitte | Alexanderplatz 5 | www.houseofweekend.berlin | U-/S Alexanderplatz*

LIDO ★ (154 B3) *(∅ N6)*
This self-proclaimed "rock-indie-electro-pop living room" puts on regular concerts. The Karrera Klub night for indie fans is now a cornerstone of the Berlin scene, and comes to Lido several times a month. *Opening times and admission depending on programme, parties from 11pm | Kreuzberg | Cuvrystr. 7 | tel. 030 69 56 68 40 | www.lido-berlin.de | U 1 Schlesisches Tor*

PRINCE CHARLES (153 D5) *(∅ L5)*
This club was founded on the site of the converted Bechstein piano factory, occupying the former employee swimming pool. The music ranges from electro to hip-hop, with regular concerts and readings. If you need a bite to eat visit the neighbouring restaurant *Parker Bowles*. *Thu–Sat 9pm–7am | admission 8–10 euros | Kreuzberg | Prinzenstr. 85f | www. princecharlesberlin.de | U 8 Moritzplat*

Live music at the Quasimodo

QUASIMODO (139 D4) *(∅ F5)*
Traditional jazz club with concerts by well-known musicians. Almost all of the world-famous funk, soul and jazz stars – from Defunkt to Jasper van't Hof – have played here. *Daily from 9pm | admission 15–22 euros | Charlottenburg | Kantstr. 12a | tel. 030 3 12 80 86 | www.quasimodo.de | U/S Zoologischer Garten*

SALON ZUR WILDEN RENATE
(155 D3) *(∅ P6)*
A club with a strict door policy and a relaxed lounge atmosphere. Boasts multiple small floors playing everything from techno to cosmic disco. *Fri/Sat from*

around midnight | admission 10 euros | Friedrichshain | tel. 030 25041426 | www.renate.cc | S Treptower Park

SPINDLER & KLATT IN DER HEERESBÄCKEREI (154 A2) (*∅ N5*)

Club restaurant with lounge atmosphere and a touch of Asia in an old warehouse. So stylish even George Clooney was here. Lovely terrace on the Spree. *Dinner Thu– Sat from 8pm, in the summer daily from 7pm, club Fri/Sat from 11pm | admission 10 euros | Kreuzberg | Köpenicker Str. 16-17 | tel. 030 3 19 88 18 60 | www.spindlerklatt. com | U1 Schlesisches Tor*

TRESOR (153 E3) (*∅ M5*)

International techno DJs sit at the turntables in this former heating plant. A 30 m (110 ft) long tunnel leads to the dance floor in the cellar. Rough industrial atmosphere and the noise level is nothing for sensitive souls. *Mon, Wed, Fri/Sat from midnight | admission 7–15 euros | Mitte | Köpenicker Str. 70 | tel. 030 62 90 87 50 | www. tresorberlin.de | U8 Heinrich-Heine-Straße*

WATERGATE ☆ (154 B2–3) (*∅ N5–6*)

Inside a former office building overlooking the Spree is a nightclub playing house and techno music across two floors, with views of the Oberbaum Bridge. During the summer you can sit on the jetty and dip your feet in the water. *Wed, Fri/Sat from midnight | admission 10–15 euros | Kreuzberg | Falckensteinstr. 49 | tel. 030 61 28 03 94 | www.water-gate.de | U1 Schlesisches Tor*

SHOWS & CABARET

BAR JEDER VERNUNFT ★ (139 E6) (*∅ F6*)

It is worth visiting this cabaret just to see the extravagant Art Nouveau mirror tent. But, the innovative programme with stars from the chanson and comedy world also have a lot going for them. You can eat

An atmospheric setting for cabaret, music and variety performances: Tipi am Kanzleramt

and during the performance. *Box office Mon–Sat noon–6:30pm, Sun 3–5:30pm, door from 6:30pm | tickets 19–75 euros| Wilmersdorf | Schaperstr. 24 | tel. 030 8 83 15 82 | www.bar-jeder-vernunft. de | U 1, 9 Spichernstraße*

DIE STACHELSCHWEINE
(139 E–F4) *(ﾉﾉ G5)*

This political cabaret full of wit and verve is an institution in West Berlin. *Tickets 22–37 euros | Charlottenburg| Tauentzienstr. 9 | Europa-Center | tel. 030 2 61 47 95 | www.diestachelschweine.de | U 9, 15 Kurfürstendamm*

DISTEL (140 C3) *(ﾉﾉ K3–4)*

An East Berlin institution for more than 60 years. While the Wall was still standing its performers were masters at covertly criticising the East German system. Today, German politics is the target of their irony. *Box office Mon–Fri 11am–6pm, Sat/Sun 11am–5pm | tickets 15–35 euros | Mitte | Friedrichstr. 101 | tel. 030 2 04 47 04 | U/S Friedrichstraße*

TIPI AM KANZLERAMT (151 E2) *(ﾉﾉ H4)*

Well-known entertainment stars such as Georgette Dee and Tim Fischer appear here as do up-and-coming a-cappella-ensembles and virtuoso African drummers. Rustic atmosphere in a marquee next to the Federal Chancellery. Tickets 20–60 euros. *Tiergarten | Große Querallee | ticket tel. 030 39 06 65 50 | www.tipi-am-kanzler amt.de | U/S Brandenburger Tor*

INSIDER TIP ► UFA-FABRIK
(165 D4) *(ﾉﾉ J10)*

The whole universe of off-culture on the former premises of the UFA film company: a circus for children to take part in, cabaret, variety shows. *Tempelhof | Viktoriastr. 10–18 | tel. 030 75 50 30 | www.ufafabrik.de | U6 Ullsteinstraße*

CINEMAS

The approximately 300 cinemas offer everything from American blockbusters to Polish experimental films, some in their original language. You can find a list of what is showing in the Berlin events magazines *Zitty* and *Tip* as well as online: *www.berlin.de/kino.*

PUBS

ALOIS S. (147 E3) *(ﾉﾉ M1)*

Traditional tavern with a beer garden that serves tapas alongside Augustiner beers. Meeting point for Werder Bremen fans on match days, while parents will appreciate the small playground next to the terrace. *Mon–Fri from 3pm (in the winter from 6pm), Sat from 1pm (2), Sun from 11am (4pm) | Prenzlauer Berg | Senefelder Str. 18 | tel. 030 44 71 96 80 | www.aloiss.de | S Prenzlauer Allee*

BÖTZOW-PRIVAT (152 B1) *(ﾉﾉ K3)*

Classic corner bar with dark wooden furniture that is also popular among young creative types from the surrounding galleries. Serves home-brewed beer and traditional fare. *Mon–Fri from 5:30pm, Sat/Sun from noon | Mitte | Linienstr. 113 | tel. 030 28 09 53 90 | www.boetzow-privat.de | S 1, 2, 25 Oranienburger Straße*

LEMKE (141 E2) *(ﾉﾉ L3)*

The rustic brewery in railway arch 143 offers a lot of different beers and hearty food from the grill. Beer garden in summer. *Daily from noon | Mitte | S-Bahnbogen 143 | tel. 030 24 72 87 27 | www.brauhaus-lemke.de | S Hackescher Markt*

MÖBEL OLFE (153 E5) *(ﾉﾉ M6)*

This social housing estate in the heart of Kreuzberg, close to Kottbusser Tor, is home to an institution of Berlin's queer scene (though it also welcomes straight visitors). Well-worn sofas, 20 varieties of Polish vodka, and a relaxed smoking policy. *Tue–Sun from 6pm | Kreuzberg | Reichenberger Str. 177 | tel. 030 23 27 46 90 | www.moebel-olfe.de | U1, 8 Kottbusser Tor*

RESTAURATION SOPHIEN 11

(141 E1) (*ΩＬ3*)

Comfy pub with an inner courtyard next to the Hackesche Höfe where you can relax over reasonably-priced meatballs and beer. *Sun–Tue 4pm–midnight, Wed–Sat noon–midnight | Mitte | Sophienstr. 11 | tel. 030 2 83 21 36 | www.restauration-sophien11.de | S Hackescher Markt*

INSIDER TIPP SCHILLERKLAUSE

(149 F4) (*Ω F5*)

One-of-a-kind West Berlin institution near the Schiller Theatre. The walls are papered with actors' autographs, and together with the dim lighting and cheap beer they give the place a wonderfully authentic atmosphere. You can also tuck into a substantial buffet for 8 euros. *Daily from 2pm, in the winter from 4pm | Charlottenburg | Schillerstr. 10 | tel. 030 3 13 59 96 | www.schillerklause.de | U 2 Ernst-Reuter-Platz*

STÄNDIGE VERTRETUNG

(140 B3) (*Ω K3–4*)

When the government moved to Berlin, many people from the Rhineland came with it. This is where lively exiled Bonners (even VIPs) get together for a glass of Kölsch beer and celebrate carnival the way they did it back home. Berliners tend to avoid it, though… *Daily 10:30am–1am | Mitte | Schiffbauerdamm 8 | tel. 030 2 82 39 65 | U/S Friedrichstraße*

YORCKSCHLÖSSCHEN ● (160 A1) (*Ω J6*)

A bit run-down but still cosy is how regulars swigging their beer or listening to a live concert (fee 4–8 euros) feel about this place. Lovely beer garden in summer. One of the oldest jazz pubs in the city. *Mon–Sat 5pm–3am, Sun from 10am | Kreuzberg | Yorckstr. 15 | tel. 030 20 15 80 70 | www.yorckschloesschen.de | U 6, 7 Mehringdamm*

CONCERTS, MUSICALS, DANCE & OPERA

ADMIRALSPALAST (140 C3) (*Ω K3–4*)

The entertainment palace from 1911 is one of the few from this time that still has life in it: shows, musicals and concerts. *Mitte | Friedrichstr. 101 | tel. 030 47 99 74 99 | U/S Friedrichstraße*

DEUTSCHE OPER (138 A2) (*Ω E4*)

Once the West's answer to the Staatsoper in the East. Today, a house with unconventional interpretations. *Charlottenburg | Bismarckstr. 35 | tel. 030 34 38 43 43 | www.deutscheoperberlin.de | U 2 Deutsche Oper*

DOCK 11 (146 C4) (*Ω L2*)

The only Berlin stage that focuses on dance all year round. The productions change on a weekly basis. Also dance lessons. *Prenzlauer Berg | Kastanienallee 79 | tel. 030 4 48 12 22 | www.dock11-berlin.de | tram 12, M1 Schwedter Straße*

FRIEDRICHSTADT-PALAST ★

(140 C2) (*Ω K3*)

Germany's only – and the world's largest – revue theatre with plenty of high-kicking dancing girls. *Mitte | Friedrichstr. 107 | tel. 030 23 26 23 26 | www.palast.berlin | U 6 Oranienburger Tor*

GRIPS THEATER (139 F1) (*Ω G4*)

A Berlin institution that shows socio-critical musicals for the city's youth. Volker Ludwig's musical set in the underground "Linie 1" has been playing for 30 years.

Excellent acoustics: concert hall of the Philharmonic Orchestra

Moabit | Altonaer Str. 22 / in the Hansaplatz underground station | tel. 030 3 97 47 40 | www.grips-theater.de | U 9 Hansaplatz

HEBBEL AM UFER (152 B6) *(ᴍ K6)*

Experimental concept focussing mainly on dance on three stages. *Kreuzberg | HAU 1 (Stresemannstr. 29) | HAU 2 (Hallesches Ufer 32), HAU 3 (Tempelhofer Ufer 10) | tel. 030 25 90 04 27 | www.hebbel-am-ufer. de | U 1, 6 Hallesches Tor*

KONZERTHAUS AM GENDARMENMARKT (141 D5) *(ᴍ K4)*

Today, the Konzerthausorchester is the main performer in what was originally a theatre built by Schinkel between 1818 and 1821. One drawback, however, the acoustics are not ideal everywhere. *Advance sales Mon–Sat noon–7pm, Sun noon–4pm | Mitte | Am Gendarmenmarkt 2 | tel. 030 2 03 09 21 01 | www.konzert haus.de | U 2, 6 Stadtmitte*

INSIDER TIP ▶ NEUKÖLLNER OPER (165 D4) *(ᴍ N8)*

Comparatively small theatre with amusing performances and unconventional interpretations of light operas and musical plays. A real off-opera! *Neukölln | Karl-Marx-Str. 131–133 | tel. 030 68 89 07 77 | www.neukoellneroper.de | U 7 Karl-Marx-Straße*

PHILHARMONIE ★ (151 E4) *(ᴍ J5)*

This is the home of the Berlin Philharmonic Orchestra and its conductor Sir Simon Rattle (who will be succeeded in 2019 by Kirill Petrenko). The acoustics in the building designed by Hans Scharoun are first-rate. ● INSIDER TIP ▶ Free concerts at 1pm on Tuesdays from September to June! *Advance sales Mon–Fri 3–6pm, Sat/Sun 11am–2pm | Tiergarten | Herbert-von-Karajan-Str. 1 | tel. 030 25 48 89 99 | www. berliner-philharmoniker.de | U/S Potsdamer Platz*

STAATSOPER UNTER DEN LINDEN
(141 D4) (*ɰ K4*)

Berlin's oldest opera is back again after extensive refurbishments. The impressive main hall shows big opera and ballet productions. *Mitte | Unter den Linden 7 | ticket booth daily 11am–7pm | tel. 030 20 35 45 55 | www.staatsoper-berlin. de | U 6 Französische Straße*

THEATER DES WESTENS
(139 D4) (*ɰ F5*)

Musical theatre. The house opened in the 19th century and many stars, including Josephine Baker and Hildegard Knef, have performed here. *Charlottenburg | Kantstr. 12 | ticket hotline tel. 01805*

44 44 (*) *| www.stage-entertainment. de | U/S Zoologischer Garten*

DANCE

GRÜNER SALON
(141 F1) (*ɰ L3*)

Tuesday night is salsa time in a side wing of the Volksbühne theatre with open classes *(8–9pm, 8 euros)*, after that it's party time. Concertson the other days. *Mitte | Rosa-Luxemburg-Platz 2 | tel. 030 24 00 93 27 | www.gruener-salon.de | U 2 Rosa-Luxemburg-Platz*

HAVANNA (159 D3) (*ɰ H7*)

Dance, dance, dance: Latin and Black Music on four Floors. One hour before the regular openig time, you can take part in a INSIDER TIPP dance class (e.g. salsa: 5 euros including admission). *Wed from 9pm, Fri/Sat from 10pm | Schöneberg | Hauptstr. 30 | tel. 030 784 85 65 | www. havanna-berlin.de | U 7 Kleistpark*

SPOTLIGHT ON SPORTS

Football fans head for the *Olympia-stadium* that was renovated for the 2006 World Championship (see p. 55). This is where the professionals from *Hertha BSC* play. There are fan shops in all major department stores in Berlin. Tickets online or from *tel. 030 3 00 92 8 18 92*. The main office is in the Olympia-stadium **(164 C3)** (*ɰ A4*) *(Charlotten-burg | Hanns-Braun-Str. | Friesenhaus II | tel. 030 30 68 81 00 (*) | www.her thabsc.de)*. The second-league team *FC Union (www.fc-union-berlin.de)* plays in the *An der Alten Försterei* sta-dium **(165 E4)** (*ɰ O*) out in the Wuhl-heide park in Köpenick. Tickets can be

purchased at most booking offices as well as online. The national-league basketball team *Alba Berlin (www.al-baberlin.de)* is a must if you are inter-ested in the sport. Home games are played in the *Mercedes Benz Arena* **(154 B2)** (*ɰ N5*) *(Mühlenstr. 12–30)* at Ostbahnhof. This is also the home of ice hockey pros *Polar Bears Berlin (www. eisbaeren.de)*. Tickets for both teams: *tel: 01806 57 00 11 (*)*. First-rate hand-ball is played by the *Füchse Berlin (www. fuechse.berlin)* in the *Max-Schmeling-Halle* **(146 C3)** (*ɰ L1*) *(Prenzlauer Berg | Am Falkplatz 1)*. Tickets online and at many ticket offices.

THEATRE

BERLINER ENSEMBLE
(140 B–C2) (*J–K3*)

This is where Bertolt Brecht used to work. His plays are still a staple of its repertoire. However, the new director Oliver Reese – who replaced Claus Peynmann at the end of his 18-year term in summer 2017 – plans to introduce more contemporary theatre. Popular; often sold out. *Mitte | Bertolt-Brecht-Platz 1 | tel. 030 28 40 81 55 | www.berliner-ensemble.de | U/S Friedrichstraße*

DEUTSCHES THEATER ⭐
(140 B2) (*J3*)

This was Germany's most famous theatre 100 years ago when Max Reinhardt was its director. Today, the threads of a glorious past are being picked up. Many classical plays in the repertoire, but also contemporary ones. *Mitte | Schumannstr. 13a | tel. 030 28 44 12 25 | www.deutschestheater.de | U 6 Oranienburger Tor*

MAXIM GORKI THEATER
(141 D3) (*K4*)

Ambitious plays by young authors as well as classics. *Mitte | Am Festungsgraben 2 | tel. 030 20 22 11 15 | www.gorki.de | S Hackescher Markt*

SCHAUBÜHNE (149 D6) (*E6*)

This former cinema on Lehniner Platz is home to politically and socially engaged theatre under the supervision of artistic director Thomas Ostermeier, and is still true to the vision of the theatre's legendary founder Peter Stein. The theatre company includes German film stars such as Nina Hoss and Lars Eidinger. *Wilmersdorf | Kurfürstendamm 153 | tel. 030 89 00 23 | www.schaubuehne.de | U7 Adenauerplatz*

Sophisticated plays at the Maxim Gorki theater

INSIDER TIP SOPHIENSAELE
(141 E1) (*L3*)

One of the most important independent theatre venues in the German-speaking world, where the boundaries between performance, dance and the visual arts are frequently blurred. *Mitte | Sophienstr. 18 | tel. 030 2 83 52 66 | www.sophiensaele.com | S Hackescher Markt*

VOLKSBÜHNE (141 F1) (*L3*)

A theatre in turbulent transition. Enfant terrible Frank Castorf served as director until 2017, when he was replaced by Chris Dercon, formerly director of the Tate Modern and a newcomer to the Berlin theatre scene. Seen by some as a symbol of encroaching globalisation and homogenisation, his appointment met with fierce resistance – culminating in a 6-day occupation of the theatre by left-wing activists. *Mitte | Rosa-Luxemburg-Platz 2 | tel. 030 24 06 57 77 | www.volksbuehne-berlin.de | U 2 Rosa-Luxemburg-Platz*

WHERE TO STAY

If there is one branch in Berlin that is really booming, it is tourism. By now, there are more than 30 million overnight stay per year; almost 140,000 beds are waiting for guests.

The industry has also left its mark on the city's skyline, with hotels popping up everywhere – from architecturally impressive buildings like the Waldorf Astoria by the Memorial Church to chains such as Motel One or the latest branch of the German Youth Hostel Association at Ostkreuz. Unlike London or New York, the accommodation on offer is universally inexpensive – which only serves to attract more visitors. The State of Berlin (known to be in financial difficulties) wishes to share in the boom, and therefore introduced the city tax in 2014. This levy – similar to a

visitor's tax – amounts to five percent of the price per night, and is added on to your hotel receipt (though business trips are exempt).

Private accommodation has become particularly popular among visitors to Berlin over the last few years. Internet portals such as Airbnb and Wimdu allow people to rent rooms or entire homes at a low price, while the usual occupants stay temporarily with friends and thus earn themselves a little extra cash. A change in the law means that a licence is now required in order to rent out accommodation in this way, but this is seldom obtained in practice. If the authorities get wind of any illegal arrangements then it is only the landlord who gets fined – but guests nonetheless run

From over-the-top luxury and carefully curated design to cheap hostels – Berlin offers accommodation to suit every budget

the risk of being left without accommodation. You can find an overview of Berlin's hotel offering on the standard online booking portals, as well as on Berlin's tourist website *www.visitberlin. de (Tel. 030 25 00 23 23)*.

HOTELS: EXPENSIVE

ACKSELHAUS ⭐ (147 D5) (*M2*)
Beautifully themed rooms and apartments, a Balinese courtyard garden and a goldfish pond. To reach the rooms on the ground floor, you cross over water using stepping stones. Delightful accommodation! *35 rooms | Prenzlauer Berg | Belforter Str. 21 | tel. 030 44 33 76 33 | www.ackselhaus.de | U 2 Senefelderplatz*

BRISTOL HOTEL KEMPINSKI BERLIN
(139 D5) (*F5*)
The classic on Kurfürstendamm. After a stroll through the city, its guests can relax in great comfort. It also has Berlin's largest Presidential Suite on two floors. *301 rooms and suites |*

Ready for an elevator ride in an aquarium? Go to the Radisson Blue

Charlottenburg | Kurfürstendamm 27 | tel. 030 88 43 40 | www.kempinski-berlin.de | U 1 Uhlandstraße

THE MANDALA HOTEL (151 F4) (*M J5*)

A privately run design hotel with stylish, minimalist décor. The restaurant *Facil* boasts two Michelin stars. *158 studios and suites | Mitte | Potsdamer Str. 3 | tel. 030 90 05 00 00 | www.themandala.de | U/S Potsdamer Platz*

NHOW ★ (154 B–C2) (*M N–O5*)

Many creative guests are attracted by Karim Rashid's cool design and the fact that sound studios can be rented. The retro-futuristic interior of the hotel's *Fabrics* restaurant on the banks of the Spree reminds one of a mixture between Alice in Wonderland and Star Trek. *304 rooms | Friedrichshain | Stralauer Allee 3 | tel. 030 2 90 29 90 | www.nh-hotels.de | U/S Warschauer Straße*

Q! (138 C5) (*M L3*)

Sweeping lounge design – even the reception looks like a cocktail bar. Award-winning and widely acclaimed, exquisite thai cuisine in the *Fox Bar. 72 rooms, 4 studios, 1 penthouse | Charlottenburg | Knesebeckstr. 67 | tel. 030 8 10 06 60 | www.hotel-q.com | U 1 Uhlandstraße*

RADISSON BLU (141 E3) (*M L4*)

The five-star hotel is located on the banks of the Spree directly opposite Berliner Dom. The largest cylindrical aquarium in the world with a million litres of water is located in the lobby. A lift from the Sea-Life Aquarium passes through the underwater world up to the sixth floor. *427 rooms | Mitte | Karl-Liebknecht-Str. 3 | tel. 030 23 82 80 | www.berlin.radissonblu.com | S Hackescher Markt*

TITANIC DELUXE (141 D4) (*M K4*)

A luxury hotel installed in a building formerly owned by the Berlin State Opera with the addition of 600 tonnes of marble, this place offers a touch of the Orient with its own Turkish bath. The name refers to the scale of the luxury on offer, of course – not to the well-known nautical disaster... *208 rooms/suites | Mitte | Französische Str. 30 | tel. 030 20 14 37 08 00 | www.titanic.com.tr | U 6 Französische Straße*

25HOURS BERLIN ★ (139 F4) (*⁄⁄⁄ G5*)
Creatively styled rooms, free bike and mini hire. The excellent bar on the 10th floor and the good *Neni* restaurant lure not only hotel guests to the city's west. *149 rooms | Charlottenburg | Budapester Str. 40 | tel. 030 30120 2210 | www.25hours-hotels.com | U 1, 2, 3 Wittenbergplatz*

HOTELS: MODERATE

AMANO (152 C1) (*⁄⁄⁄ L3*)
Central location, roof terrace, bright rooms with soundproof windows – stay in style between the Hackesche Markt and Rosenthaler Platz. Tip: the *Amano Bar* diagonally opposite. *117 rooms | Mitte | Auguststr. 43 | tel. 030 8094150 | www.amanogroup.de | U 8 Rosenthaler Platz*

ARTE LUISE KUNSTHOTEL
(140 A–B 2–3) (*⁄⁄⁄ J3*)
Each room has been individually decorated by a different artist, getting you in the mood for Berlin's cultural scene. But comfort and homeliness also get their due. *50 rooms | Mitte | Luisenstr. 19 | tel. 030 28 44 80 | www.luise-berlin.com | U/S Friedrichstraße*

GARDEN LIVING ★ (140 A1) (*⁄⁄⁄ J3*)
Live like in a Roman palazzo; its inner courtyard blossoms in summer with a fountain, palm trees, orange bushes and veranda to enjoy a leisurely breakfast. The rooms are furnished in wood and warm colours – in pleasant contrast to the grey skies over Berlin. *27 rooms/ apartments | Mitte | Invalidenstr. 101 | tel. 030 28445590 | www.gardenliving. de | U 6 Naturkundemuseum*

INSIDER TIP **HOTEL STADTBAD ODERBERGER** (147 D4) (*⁄⁄⁄ L2*)
A few details in the modern rooms point to the fact that the building was originally opened 100 years ago as a public bathhouse. The 20 m/66ft pool is a historic monument, open to hotel guests and

---

★ **Michelberger Hotel**
International stars have been known to give impromptu concerts at this hip hotel → p. 102

★ **Ku' Damm 101**
A reasonably priced and centrally located design hotel → p. 103

★ **Nhow**
Top designer hotel with interiors by Karim Rashid → p. 100

★ **Heart of Gold Hostel**
The Berlin Mitte party scene is not far away; light and quiet rooms for the not-so-well-off → p. 104

★ **25hours Berlin**
Creatively furnished hotel, designed as a big city jungle – the zoo is right next door → p. 101

★ **Ackselhaus**
Exotic: flats with a goldfish pond and Balinese garden → p. 99

★ **Miniloft Mitte**
Spectacular architecture, friendly service → p. 105

★ **Garden Living**
Lovingly furnished boutique hotel with beautiful atrium and personal service → p. 101

MARCO POLO HIGHLIGHTS

local residents. *72 rooms, 5 suites | Prenzlauer Berg | Oderberger Str. 57–59 | tel. 030 7 80 08 97 60 | www.hotel-oderberger.berlin | U 2 Eberswalder Straße*

also where readings are held. Personal atmosphere. *18 rooms | Friedenau | Fregestr. 68 | tel. 030 8 59 09 60 | www.literaturhotel-berlin.de | S1, 25 Friedenau*

DAS LITERATURHOTEL
(158 C5) (*Ø G8*)

Books decorate the walls of the breakfast room furnished with antiques. This is

MICHELBERGER HOTEL ★
(154 B2) (*Ø N5*)

A hip hotel boasting individual décor, with loft rooms spanning two floors.

LUXURY HOTELS

Adlon Kempinski (140 B4) (*Ø J7*)
Perfectly presented contemporary interpretation of the luxury hotel on the same site that was destroyed in the war. Impeccable service. *304 rooms, 78 suites | 236–12,500 euros | Mitte | Unter den Linden 77 | tel. 030 2 26 10 | www.hotel-adlon.de | S 1, 2, 25 Brandenburger Tor*

Grand Hyatt (151 F4) (*Ø J5*)
The five star hotel at the Potsdamer Platz is characterized by its simple elegance and modern interior. Highlight is the ☀ wellness landscape on the top floor with a high grade steel pool and best view of the city. *342 rooms and suites | 160–9,750 euros | Tiergarten | Marlene-Dietrich-Platz 2 | tel. 030 25 53 12 34 | www.berlin.grand.hyatt.de | U/S Potsdamer Platz*

Waldorf Astoria (139 E4) (*Ø F5*)
Highest standards of service in the new skyscraper at the Gedächtniskirche. With a Guerlain spa, the gourmet restaurant *Les Solistes, Romanisches Café* and *Peacock Gallery Bar.* 182 rooms, 50 suites | 189–10,000 euros | Charlottenburg | Hardenbergstr. 28 | tel. 030 8 14 00 00 | www.waldorfastoria.com | U /S Zoologischer Garten*

Hotel de Rome (141 D4) (*Ø K4*)
Temple of luxury next to the Staatsoper on Bebelplatz. The rooms and suites are modern with a touch of traditional Berlin architecture. Beautiful ☀ rooftop terrace with bar. *146 rooms and suites | 295–7,000 euros | Mitte | Behrenstr. 37 | tel. 030 4 60 60 90 | www.hotelderome.com | U 6 Französische Straße*

The Ritz-Carlton Berlin (140 A6) (*Ø J5*)
Top-class hotel, centrally-located at Potsdamer Platz: stately, large spa complex with indoor pool and luxury wherever you look. *303 rooms and suites | 205–14,500 euros | Mitte | Potsdamer Platz 3 | tel. 030 33 77 77 | www.ritzcarlton.com | U/S Potsdamer Platz*

Schlosshotel im Grunewald (156 B4) (*Ø C7*)
Historical palace with palace gardens. Spa facilities and gourmet restaurant. The interior was designed by Karl Lagerfeld. *53 rooms and suites | 260–5,800 euros | Wilmersdorf | Brahmsstr. 10 | tel. 030 89 58 40 | www.schlosshotelberlin.com | S 7, 9 Grunewald*

Revival of a traditional address at the Brandenburger Tor: Hotel Adlon

Travis and Damien Rice have held concerts in the courtyard here. *100 rooms | Friedrichshain | Warschauer Str. 39–40 | tel. 030 29 77 85 90 | michelbergerhotel. com | U/S Warschauer Straße*

HOTELS: BUDGET

FABRIK (154 B3) (*N6*)
Ideal for fans of the Kreuzberg nightlife, as they can fall into bed after a night out. Prices start at 18 euros, depending on room size. *45 rooms | Kreuzberg | Schlesische Str. 18 | tel. 030 6 11 82 54 | www. diefabrik.com | U 1 Schlesisches Tor*

KARIBUNI (165 D4) (*N7*)
Family-run hotel in a typical old Berlin building with furniture and wall paintings inspired by Africa. In East Africa, *karibuni* means "welcome". *11 rooms, 1 flat | Neukölln | Neckarstr. 2/corner of Karl-Marx-Str. | tel. 030 6 87 15 17 | www.ka ribuni-hotel.de | U 7 Rathaus Neukölln*

KU' DAMM 101 ★ (157 D1) (*D6*)
A minimalist design hotel with an urban garden, aroma steam bath, and rooms starting at 64 euros. *169 rooms | Halensee | Kurfürstendamm 101 | tel. 030 5 20 05 50 | www.kudamm101.com | S 41, 42, 46*

MOTEL ONE (139 D4) (*F5*)
Designer hotel with reasonably-priced rooms. Other branches are located at the main railway station and on Alexanderplatz (Mitte), on Moritzplatz (Kreuzberg) and near Schloss Bellevue (Tiergarten). *250 rooms | Charlottenburg | Kantstr. 7–11a | tel. 030 315 17 73 60 | www.motel-one.com | S 7, 9, 75 Zoologischer Garten*

PENSION PETERS (138 C4) (*F5*)
Comfortable rooms for non-smokers – and also families – in one of Berlins typical old buildings near Savignyplatz. Many good cafés and restaurants in the vicinity. *34 rooms | Charlottenburg | Kantstr. 146 |*

Hüttenpalast: original accommodation in indoor caravans

tel. 030 3 12 22 78 | www.pension-peters-berlin.de | S Savignyplatz

HOSTELS

CIRCUS HOSTEL (146 C6) (*M L3*)
Stylish hostel with a micro-brewery in the cellar, located on the bustling Rosenthaler Platz. Dorm beds are available from 19 euros, and you can also hire bikes and Segways. *72 rooms | Mitte | Weinbergsweg 1a | tel. 030 20 00 39 39 | www.circus-berlin.de | U 8 Rosenthaler Platz*

EASTERN COMFORT (154 B2) (*M N5*)
Two small hotel ships along the Oberbaumbrücke near the Eastside Gallery offer you the opportunity to spend a night on the Spree, with a view through the bulls eyes included. (15–78 euros per night). *42 cabins | Friedrichshain | Mühlenstr. 73–77 | tel. 030 66 76 38 06 | www.eastern-comfort.com | U/S Warschauer Straße*

EASTSEVEN (147 D5) (*M L2*)
Elected "Germany's best hostel" in 2015. The bedrooms are all decorated with murals and have their own bathrooms. Party groups are not welcome! Quiet garden. *60 beds | Prenzlauer Berg | Schwedter Str. 7 | tel. 030 93 62 22 40 | www.eastseven.de | U 2 Senefelderplatz*

HEART OF GOLD HOSTEL ⭐
(140 C2) (*M K3*)
Rooms that were inspired by Douglas Adams' iconic novel (and film) The Hitchhiker's Guide to the Galaxy, from 9.90 euros, near the Museumsinsel. *140 rooms | Mitte | Johannisstr. 11 | tel. 030 29 00 33 00 | www.heartofgold-hostel.de | U 6 Oranienburger Tor*

INSIDER TIP HÜTTENPALAST
(161 F 1–2) (*M M7*)
Funny and convenient: camping in a factory hall in Neukölln. Let one of the three caravans or the three wooden huts harbour you. Nice café and garden terrace. Also a family room. *Neukölln | Hobrechtstr. 65–66 | tel. 030 37 30 58 06 | www.huettenpalast.de | U 7, 8 Hermannplatz*

OSTEL (154 A–B1) (*N5*)

If you want to experience a bit of GDR feeling: hotel in a prefabricated house with authentic East German furniture and the obligatory Honecker portrait in the foyer. Easily accessible location near the Ostbahnhof. The in-house restaurant *Volkskammer* serves original GDR cuisine. *79 rooms, 1 flat | Friedrichshain | Wriezener Karree 5 | tel. 030 25 76 86 60 | www.ostel.eu | S 7, 8, 9 Ostbahnhof*

INSIDER TIP PFEFFERBETT
(147 D5) (*L2*)

Beautiful dormitories in a former Berlin brewery (from 12 euros). A double room with your own bathroom, TV and internet access costs approx. 80 euros. *43 beds, 3 flats | Prenzlauer Berg | Christinenstr. 18–19 | tel. 030 93 93 58 58 | www.pfefferbett.de | U 2 Senefelderplatz*

THREE LITTLE PIGS (152 A5) (*J5*)

You can stay in two to eight-bed rooms in a converted monastery near Potsdamer Platz. Double room from 65 euros. *80 rooms | Kreuzberg | Stresemannstr. 66 | tel. 030 26 39 58 80 | www.three-little-pigs.de | U/S Potsdamer Platz*

FLATS

GORKI APARTMENTS (146 C6) (*L2*)

Guests here are assigned their own doorbell nameplates and letterboxes, in a bid to make you feel more at home. Cosy-yet-stylish apartments, with staff clad in Danish designer uniforms. *34 flats, 2 penthouses | Mitte | Weinbergsweg 25 | tel. 030 48 49 64 80 | www.gorkiapartments.com | U 8 Rosenthaler Platz | Expensive*

MINILOFT MITTE ★
(140 B1) (*J3*)

Prize-winning architecture with an impressive glass façade near the main station where you can choose between flats that are classically or extravagantly furnished. Personal, cordial service. Environmentally-friendly operation with eco-electricity and fair-trade products. *14 flats | Mitte | Hessische Str. 5 | tel. 030 8 47 10 90 | www.miniloft.com | U 6 Naturkundemuseum | Moderate*

PRIVATE ROOMS

The city authorities declared war on holiday apartments in residential buildings a few years ago in a bid to combat the city's housing shortage; however, you can still find offers, such as on *www.ferienwohnungen-berlin.de*.

LOW BUDGET

If all you want is a sofa to sleep on then give *www.couchsurfing.com* a try. Participants generally pay for their homestay accommodation by offering their own sofa on the platform in return.

Brand new: *Berlin Ostkreuz Youth Hostel* **(155 D2)** (*P5*) (445 beds | Rummelsburg | Marktstr. 9–12 | tel. 030 2 00 50 92-0 | www.jugendherbergeberlinostkreuz.de | S Ostkreuz) Bed from 25 euros.

In the *Pension 11. Himmel* **(165 E3)** (*0*) (5 rooms | Wittenberger Str. 85 | tel. 030 93 77 20 52 | www.pension-11himmel.de | S 7 Ahrensfelde) in a prefabricated concrete building in Marzahn, you can either sleep in a hammock or a prince's bed. One night with breakfast from 18 euros.

DISCOVERY TOURS

1   BERLIN AT A GLANCE

START: ❶ Reichstag building
END: ⓰ Riva bar

1 day
Walking time
(without stops)
approx. 2½ hours

Distance:
 26.5 km/16.5 miles, of which approx.
11 km/6.8 miles on foot

COSTS: approx. 50 euros for a day ticket on the public transport network, Segway hire and snacks

 IMPORTANT TIPS: Buy a one-day BVG ticket (currently 7 euros for zones A/B) to travel for free on all buses, underground and district line trains.
Reserve a table in the Dachgartenrestaurant Käfer in advance.
Pre-book tickets online for the Fernsehturm on the ⑪ Alexanderplatz!

Would you like to explore the places that are unique to this city? Then the Discovery Tours are just the thing for you – they include terrific tips for stops worth making, breathtaking places to visit, selected restaurants and fun activities. It's even easier with the Touring App: download the tour with map and route to your smartphone using the QR Code on pages 2/3 or from the website address in the footer below – and you'll never get lost again even when you're offline.

TOURING APP

→ p. 2/3

This tour offers you a first insight into the capital's diversity: it takes you from the government quarters to colourful Kreuzberg and from Brandenburger Tor onto the Fernsehturm (television tower). Although it requires endurance, you will be rewarded with having seen a lot of Berlin.

09:30am The best place to start the day is in **Dachgartenrestaurant Käfer** → p. 67 at the top of the ❶ **Reichstag building** → p. 46 (advance reservation essential). From here, you will have a magnificent view over the inner city and can also follow the walkway up into the dome of the building. Hire

❶ Reichstag building

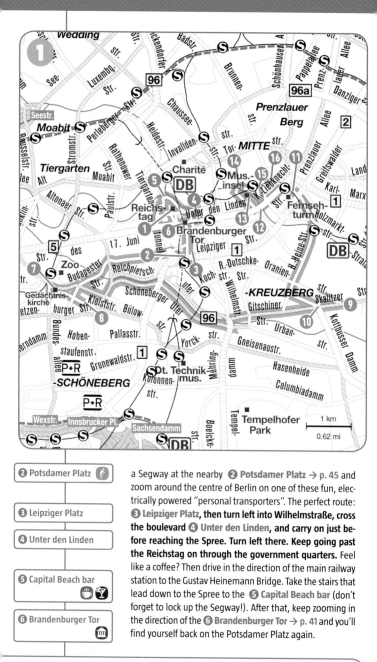

2 Potsdamer Platz 🛴	a Segway at the nearby **2 Potsdamer Platz** → p. 45 and zoom around the centre of Berlin on one of these fun, electrically powered "personal transporters". The perfect route: **3 Leipziger Platz**, then turn left into Wilhelmstraße, cross the boulevard **4 Unter den Linden**, and carry on just before reaching the Spree. Turn left there. Keep going past the Reichstag through the government quarters. Feel like a coffee? Then drive in the direction of the main railway station to the Gustav Heinemann Bridge. Take the stairs that lead down to the Spree to the **5 Capital Beach bar** (don't forget to lock up the Segway!). After that, keep zooming in the direction of the **6 Brandenburger Tor** → p. 41 and you'll find yourself back on the Potsdamer Platz again.
3 Leipziger Platz	
4 Unter den Linden	
5 Capital Beach bar ☕🍸	
6 Brandenburger Tor 🏛	

11:30am Bus no. 200 will take you past the diplomatic district to the Breitscheidplatz with the **7** **Gedächtniskirche (memorial church)** → p. 54 and the Tauentzienstraße with its many shops. Here on the **8** **Wittenbergplatz** with its splendid weekly market *(Tue 8am–2pm, Fri 8am–4pm)* is the exclusive department store KaDeWe → p. 82. Take a lunchtime break on the **INSIDER TIP** gourmet floor and later take a closer look at the enormous selection in the delicatessen and clothing.

01:30pm How about a tour of Kreuzberg? **The bus M 29 will take you there right from KaDeWe.** Get off at **9** **Görlitzer Bahnhof** and take a stroll past the wild mixture of bars, boutiques and döner kebab stands between Oranienplatz and Wiener Straße. **From "Görli" work your way down Oranienstraße** where you will come across many shops selling fashion items by Berlin designers as well as Turkish bakeries.

03:00pm At the **10** **Kottbusser Tor** get into the U8 that takes you from Kreuzberg to **11** **Alexanderplatz** → p. 34. The "Alex"'s main attraction is the Berlin **Fernsehturm (TV tower)** → p. 34 with its 203 m (666 ft) high viewing platform. Take the express lift and let it catapult you up the tower in just 40 seconds. Book your tickets online in advance without any queuing time! **From the "Alex", it is just a stone's throw on foot west along the Karl-Liebknecht-Straße** to the **12** **Schlossplatz** with the almost finished Humboldt-Forum in the restored palace and to the **13** **Museumsinsel** → p. 38, the mecca within Berlin's museum landscape. Art-lovers will be fascinated by the enormous exhibition building with valuable art collections and archaeological treasures. You should definitely plan to visit the **Neues Museum** which re-opened in 2009 with its famous Nefertiti. As it is now too late, come back another day. Due to the crowds of visitors, it is recommended to buy your ticket in advance – preferably online. During summer, treat yourself to a well-earned break **on the banks of the Spree opposite the Museumsinsel (at the Monbijou bridge)** at the **14** **Strandbar Mitte** → p. 89.

07:00pm In the **15** **Ampelmann-Restaurant** → p. 74 you can order pasta in East German "Ampelmännchen" (little traffic men) shapes as well as try some excellent international cuisine. Take a well-earned night cap at the **16** **Riva bar** → p. 89 located under the arches of the district line

- **7** Gedächtniskirche
- **8** Wittenbergplatz
- **9** Görlitzer Bahnhof
- **10** Kottbusser Tor
- **11** Alexanderplatz
- **12** Schlossplatz
- **13** Museumsinsel
- **14** Strandbar Mitte
- **15** Ampelmann-Restaurant
- **16** Riva bar

railway at the Hackescher Markt. The bar in the shape of the sunken luxury liner "Titanic" is unique and the drinks are also recommended.

2 WHERE THE WALL ONCE STOOD

START: ➊ Checkpoint Charlie
END: ⓫ Friedrichstraße

4 hours
Walking time
(without stops)
1¼ hours

Distance:
➡ 5 km/3.1 miles

COSTS: approx. 20 euros for café food and snacks

You will hardly notice that Berlin was once cut in two by a tremendous amount of cement, barbed wire and minefields. However, there are some places where you can still get an impression of how things were at the time when the city was divided. A walk along the old line of the Wall between Checkpoint Charlie and Friedrichstraße station is especially worthwhile.

➊ Checkpoint Charlie 🏛

➋ Wall 🏛

➌ Topographie des Terrors

10:00am The walk begins at the former ➊ **Checkpoint Charlie.** Only the small guard house and larger-than-life photographic portraits of Russian and American soldiers remain of what used to be the border crossing for visitors entering East Germany from the west. There is an impressive documentation of escape stories and conditions in the East and West in the **Haus am Checkpoint Charlie** → p. 52. At least 136 people attempting to escape over the Wall were killed by East German border guards. **With the stacks of sand sacks behind you, turn left into Zimmerstraße** where the Wall originally blocked the view from one side of the street to the other. When you walk **along Zimmerstraße** you will pass by houses whose occupants used to be almost in the East if they just put their hand out of the window; the Wall was not the actual border, it was a "virtual" line 2.50 m (8 ft) in front of it! This means that people walking on Zimmerstraße were really in East Berlin.

Continue along Wilhelmstraße towards the Martin Gropius Building. Here, you will see the last remnants of the almost 4-m (13 ft) high ➋ **Wall** constructed of concrete slabs. However there are a lot of holes in this section because souvenir hunters have hacked out many chunks. The ➌ **Topographie des Terrors** → p. 53 exhibition centre is located to the left. This used to be the headquarters of the

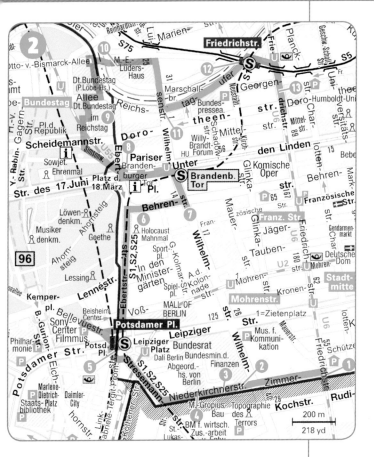

Gestapo and SS and a location of unbelievable fear and horror. There is hardly anywhere else on earth where so much terror, torture and murder was planned and carried out. A new documentation centre on the premises complements the open-air exhibition with 15 sections including one along the remains of the Wall that recalls the fate of the many victims as well as the buildings that once stood there.

Today, the ❹ **Martin-Gropius-Bau** → p. 53, the former Museum of Applied Art that was opened in 1881 and severely damaged in World War II, shows temporary exhibitions. It is named after the architect who was a great-uncle of the famous Bauhaus architect Walter Gropius. The Wall made

❹ Martin-Gropius-Bau

A labyrinth of columns at the Holocaust Memorial

it impossible to use the main entrance and visitors had to go in through the back door. The building in the style of the Italian High Renaissance opposite – on what used to be the east side of the Wall – has housed the **Berlin House of Representatives** since 1993. It was opened as the Prussian House of Representatives in 1892.

11:30am Take a look at the copper inserts in the ground; they mark the former course of the Wall. **From Stresemannstraße you can see ⑤ Potsdamer Platz → p. 45 on the right.** New buildings hide where the Wall used to be and only a copper band in the cobblestones along Stresemannstraße recalls the once-divided city. Where the skyscrapers of the German Federal Railways and Daimler Benz are today, there used to be an area of wasteland when the Wall was still standing. Until the air-raids in World War II, Potsdamer Platz was the busiest place in Europe and was also the site of Berlin's first traffic lights that were installed in 1925. This is commemorated by a tower with a clock and horizontal set of lights at the entrance to the district line station. Looking for more of a view? Then take the fastest lift in Europe to the roof of the **Kollhoff Tower → p. 45**. From there you have a fantastic view of your surroundings. The gigantic tent roof of the **Sony Center → p. 45** is flooded with coloured light emitted by thousands of LEDs after night falls. Enjoy a

⑤ Potsdamer Platz

hearty snack and try some fried chicken on the terrace of the **Lindenbräu brewery** (*Moderate*) with a fine view into the circle of this impressive building designed by Helmut Jahn.

`01:00pm` **Continue along Ebertstraße towards Pariser Platz.** The so-called Ministergärten (Minister Gardens) with the representations of numerous federal states lie on the right. This is adjacent to the Holocaust Memorial **⑥ Denkmal für die ermordeten Juden Europas** → p. 42 based on plans by the New York architect Peter Eisenman. Now it's time for a break: **Via Behren- and Wilhelmstraße you'll reach the ⑦ Altberliner Wirtshaus** (*daily from 11am* | *Wilhelmstr. 77* | *tel. 030 22 48 82 05* | *Budget*) serving hearty German fare. **Go back on Wilhelmstraße to Unter den Linden. Around the corner to the left,** and you'll stand in front of the **⑧ Brandenburger Tor**→ p. 41, where you should visit the INSIDER TIP **Raum der Stille** (Room of Silence). It is located in the northern column of the gate. It is hard to believe that before Reunification, nobody was allowed to pass through the Brandenburger Tor because it was in no-man's land between East and West. The buildings to the north of Brandenburger Tor are new even though they do not look it. **Now head off to the ⑨ Reichstag building** → p. 46, today the seat of the German Parliament. Visitors to its dome have a fantastic view over the centre of Berlin. The rays of sun flowing in through the glass dome are channelled downwards using mirrors to provide the parliament chamber beneath with natural light.

The Wall used to run behind the parliament building on the Spree side. The memorial site "Parliament of Trees against War and Violence" conceived by the Berlin environmental artist Ben Wargin in 1990, is located opposite the Reichstag in the **⑩ Marie-Elisabeth-Lüders-Haus**. Take the path along the riverbank past the **⑪ ARD-Hauptstadtstudio** (*ARD television's capital studio* | *Mitte* | *Wilhelmstr. 67a* | *tel. 030 22 88 11 10* | *www.ard-hauptstadtstudio.de*). If you are interested, take a free guided tour (*Wed, Sat 2pm*) through the studios and find out how news programmes are produced. It is now only a stone's throw to the **⑫ Friedrichstraße Station; just walk along the Spree to the east and you will reach it in five minutes.** Maybe you'd like to do some shopping? There is plenty of choice on **⑬ Friedrichstraße** with its many fashion and trendy shops and the **Dussmann** → p. 82 "culture department store".

⑥ Denkmal für die ermordeten Juden Europas

⑦ Altberliner Wirtshaus

⑧ Brandenburger Tor

⑨ Reichstag building

⑩ Marie-Elisabeth-Lüders-Haus

⑪ ARD-Hauptstadt-studio

⑫ Friedrichstraße Station

⑬ Friedrichstraße

THROUGH BERLIN'S HISTORY: THE SPANDAUER VORSTADT

START: ❶ Hackescher Markt
END: ❶ Hackescher Markt

START: ❶ Hackescher Markt **END:** ❶ Hackescher Markt	**2 hours** Walking time (without stops) 30 minutes

Distance:
🎒 **1.5 km/1 mile**

COSTS: approx. 10 euros for café food

In the 18th century, new housing was needed and the city expanded into an area that became known as the Spandauer Vorstadt – "suburban Spandau", as the road to Spandau started outside the city gates. The Scheunenviertel ("barn district") is located to the north of the Hackescher Markt district line station. In the 18th century there was a row of barns here. The "golden 20s" saw culture and crafts flourish. Many Jews – mainly from Eastern Europe – lived in the eastern part of the quarter. Today this suburb is once again seeing a resurgence of this tradition as a centre of the theatre, arts and crafts, together with shops and cafés.

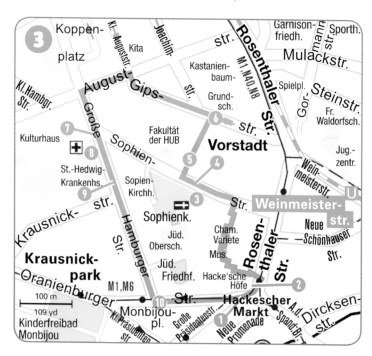

`11:00am` The **①** Hackescher Markt district line station, where our walk begins, marks the former border of the city; regional and long-distance trains travel above the foundations of the old city wall between Jannowitzbrücke and Friedrichstraße. The district line station is named after the City Commandant von Hacke who had the swampland drained in the middle of the 18th century. The **②** Hacke-sche Höfe → p. 36 opposite the square in front of the station are also named after him. The eight courtyards, one behind each other, form Europe's largest complex of this kind and now offer a great variety of fashion, culture, arts and crafts, and restaurants. **If you walk through all the courtyards you will reach** `INSIDER TIP` Sophienstraße, a spruced-up street that was renovated in the 1980s for the 750th anniversary of the city. **Going to the left, you will pass the old churchyard of the** **③** Sophienkirche after 50 m (164 ft) with the oldest Baroque church tower in the city. The **④** Handwerksvereinshaus (House of the Arts and Crafts Association) is on the right. This was built in 1844 as the gathering place of Berlin's first labour organisation. As many as 3,000 people held meetings and had discussions inside. In the 1920s in particular, Communists, Social Democrats and National Socialists held their party meetings here. A popular dance theatre with alternative-culture flair can be found at the Sophiensaele → p. 97.

A few yards further on, the route leads us through a gate-way into the **⑤** Sophie-Gips-Höfe where multimedia companies, galleries and gastronomic businesses have opened up. The American cakes in Barcomi's café (*daily until 9pm | tel. 030 28 59 83 63*) are delicious and in summer you can sit in bliss on the courtyard terrace. **The rear exit of the courtyard ensemble leads to** **⑥** Gipsstraße ("plaster street"). This is one of Spandauer Vorstadt's old-est streets. There used to be a lime kiln in the street for the production of plaster. Today it is home to many beautiful shops and studios such as from the virtuous ceramic artist Hinrich Kröger (*Gipsstr. 13 | www.galerie-hinrich-kroeger.de*) for you to gaze in the shop windows. **Go along the street on the left to the end.** The 19th/early 20th century "Gründerzeit" houses have now been renovated and it is worth taking a look into the courtyards that often still have single-storey barns.

`12:00pm` **From Auguststraße after around 50 m (164 ft) turn left onto the** **⑦** Große Hamburger Straße. In the

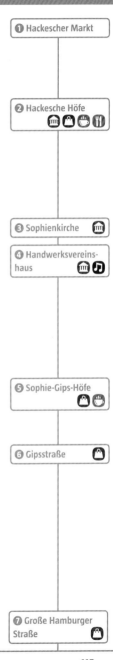

① Hackescher Markt

② Hackesche Höfe

③ Sophienkirche

④ Handwerksvereins-haus

⑤ Sophie-Gips-Höfe

⑥ Gipsstraße

⑦ Große Hamburger Straße

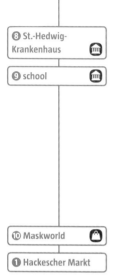

⑧ St.-Hedwig-Krankenhaus

⑨ school

⑩ Maskworld

① Hackescher Markt

1920s it was famous as a place where Jews, Protestants and Catholics lived together peacefully. There are also many shops waiting for customers. You will soon see the pretty clinker facade of **⑧ St.-Hedwig-Krankenhaus** on your right. It was opened as a hospital for the old and infirm in 1888. Diagonally opposite the hospital, the Jewish community runs a **⑨ school**. There used to be a Jewish cemetery next to the schoolyard but it was turned into a park for the former Jewish old people's home in 1827. The SS organised deportations to concentration camps from this home that no longer stands today. A memorial stone and sculpture remind us of the 56,000 Berlin Jews who were deported to Nazi death camps. **House No. 19a** opposite the former cemetery is thought to be the oldest in Spandauer Vorstadt. **Turn left onto Oranienburger Straße at the end of the street** where you can find a hive of trendy fashion stores and restaurants. Straight across from where the Große Hamburger Straße enters the Oranienburger Straße stands house number 86 A, home to **⑩ Maskworld** *(www.maskworld.com)*; with its collection of 4,000 costumes and the wildest masks on 5 floors. **After a few steps you will once again see the ① Hackescher Markt, where our tour now ends.**

4 BIKE TOUR INTO NATURE

START: ① Ahrensfelde district train station **END:** ⑪ Forum Köpenick	**4 hours** Cycling time (without stops) 1¾ hours
Distance: 🚲 19 km/11.8 miles	

COSTS: around 10 euros for café food, 8–12 euros for bike hire, 5 euros for admission to the **⑤ Gärten der Welt**, day ticket BVG 7 euros
WHAT TO TAKE: hire bike (see p. 129), climbing gear if required

The Wuhletalweg trail takes you around the city's eastern outskirts offering you both an escape into nature as well as interesting sights on both sides including Europe's largest prefabricated housing estate, the continent's largest Chinese gardens and a climbing tower built out of balustrades from demolished prefabricated buildings!

① Ahrensfelde district train station

11:00am It takes around half an hour on the S7 from Alexanderplatz to the end of the line at **① Ahrensfelde district train station**. For just a small fee, you can take the bike you have hired in the city on to the train (a bike ticket costs

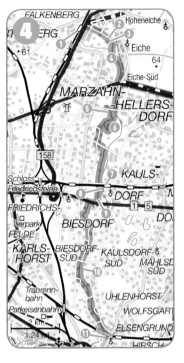

Gärten der Welt (Gardens of the World): China in Berlin

1.90 euros a journey). **Head south from the Ahrensfelde district line station along the Havemannstraße to the Wuhletal (Wuhle valley).** Shortly after the district line station you will notice brightly orange-painted three-storey buildings on your left. Hard to believe that these were once as high as the depressing eleven-storey prefabricated buildings on the opposite side of the road. At the start of the 2000s, architects were assigned with the task of transforming some of the city's high-rises into residential villas. The transformation has attracted worldwide interest. After approx. 1 km (0.6 mile), you'll welcome the green landscape of the ❷ **Wuhletal**, a floodplain marking the city's border. **Follow the signposted Wuhletalweg in a southerly direction.** Shortly after setting off you'll spot a INSIDER TIP climbing rock on the right-hand side, the so-called ❸ **Wuhletalwächter**. It was built using 550 concrete slabs taken from balconies of demolished prefab buildings from the area around and stands an impressive 17.50 m (57 ft) high. Whoever likes climbing and has the right gear with them can choose between several climbs varying

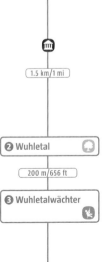

1.5 km/1 mi

❷ Wuhletal

200 m/656 ft

❸ Wuhletalwächter

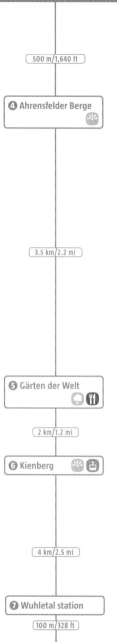

500 m/1,640 ft

④ Ahrensfelder Berge

3.5 km/2.2 mi

⑤ Gärten der Welt

2 km/1.2 mi

⑥ Kienberg

4 km/2.5 mi

⑦ Wuhletal station

100 m/328 ft

in difficulty; anyone can use the facility (at their own risk!). **100 m (320 ft) to the south of the rock** is a herd of Scottish highland cattle which have been grazing there since 2011 to keep the meadows short. In stark contrast to this are the prefabricated high-rises of Marzahn on the skyline. **After approximately 1 km (0.6 mile), the path leads you around the ④ Ahrensfelder Berge**, but if you're feeling sporty, why not try the ascent (leave the bike at the bottom or push it up) to be rewarded with an amazing view over the fields to the east and Europe's largest prefabricated housing estate to the west in Marzahn. These hills (114 and 101 m (374 ft and 331 ft) high) are higher now than they used to be (69 m (226 ft)); they were used as landfill sites up until the start of the 1990s for building rubble due to the many new prefabricated buildings built in those days.

12:00pm **The trail takes you past the wetlands of Fasanenpfuhl to the Landsberger Allee.** This is a relatively tricky section as some of the signposts directing you along the Wuhletalweg are difficult to spot. **Your route now continues on the left parallel to the Landsberger Allee. Cross the Eichener Chaussee, then the Landsberger Allee and follow the Zossener Straße for a short distance.** To the right follows another idyllic green section of your journey. **Continue along the Wuhletalweg and after approximately 1 km (0.6 mile) you'll reach the congested Eisenacher Straße.** Here is the main entrance (approx. 200 m (656 ft) on your right) to the **⑤ Gärten der Welt → p. 57**, the "Gardens of the world", with Europe's largest Chinesischer Garten. Here you can enjoy a bite to eat: The Chinese snack-bar pavilion sells drinks, salads, noodle soups and tea from the Land of the Rising Sun.

01:00pm After taking in the garden's splendid flowers, **continue on the Wuhletalweg towards ⑥ Kienberg**. This 102 m/335 ft high bump whichonly Berliners call a "mountain", is part of the garden. Highlights are a viewing platform on its "summit" and an aerial cableway. From the first, you'll have a great view of the whole garden and the Marzahn pre-fabricated building skyline in the distance. From up here you can also see the Marzahn *Flower Tower* (Allee der Kosmonauten 145), a high-rise building decorated with jungle, alpine and Mediterranean landscapes as well as Chinese flowers – Europe's highest facade artwork. **Continue** south along **the trail for 2 km (1.2 miles) past allotments and meadows to the ⑦ Wuhletal station and another 7 km (4.3 miles) to the Köpenick district line station.**

Behind the subway to the district line and underground station, **⑧ Kaulsdorf** can soon be seen on the left, a village which has retained its rural charm with its church and historical buildings.

02:00pm **After 3 km (1.8 miles) along the ⑨ Biesdorfer Höhe** (82 m/269 ft) – offering splendid views of the area around – and through a new housing estate and butterfly meadows, you will reach a splendid location to take a break at the **⑩ Wuhlesee** a lake surrounded by old trees and reeds. You can't swim here but it is an idyllic spot to take a picnic. **Head back to the Köpenick district line station (3 km (1.8 miles)) along the Wuhle** through nature and urban development. The tour ends at the shopping centre **⑪ Forum Köpenick** with a vast selection of snack bars and cafés to choose from. **The S3 line takes you back to the city centre in 25 minutes.**

| ⑧ Kaulsdorf | |

500 m/1,640 ft

| ⑨ Biesdorfer Höhe | |

3.5 km/2.2 mi

| ⑩ Wuhlesee | |

3.5 km/2.2 mi

| ⑪ Forum Köpenick | |

⑤ CRUISE THROUGH THE CITY BY SHIP

START: ❶ Spandau Citadel	**7 hours**
END: ❼ Strandbad Wannsee	Cycling time (without stops) 1¼, walking time (without stops) 1½ hours
Distance: 🚴 35 km/22 mi, of which 4 km/2.5mi on foot	

COSTS: 15 euros ship fare, 4.50 euros admission citadel, 5.50 euros admission Strandbad Wannsee, approx. 20 euros food, 7 euros BVG day ticket
WHAT TO PACK: bathing gear, sun protection, hat

IMPORTANT TIPS: The ship runs only from March to Oct (Tue–Sun); Tickets for the "7 lakes" cost 15 euros and can be bought on site. **❼ Strandbad Wannsee:** May–mid June 10am–7pm, mid June–mid Sept 9am–8pm *(www.berlinerbaeder.de)*

Every visitor to Berlin should make the effort to see it from the water – and a boat tour along the Havel shows the city off at its greenest. A preliminary visit to the Spandau Citadel offers a good overview of Berlin's long history, and you can cool off at the end of the tour with a dip in the Wannsee.

11:00am The tour begins at one of the best-preserved Renaissance fortresses in Europe: the **❶ Spandau Citadel** *(www.zitadelle-spandau.de)*. Head out of the Zitadelle U-Bahn station and cross the drawbridge to enter the 400-year-old star-shaped fortress. Climb the 30 m/98 ft **Julius Tower** for a commanding view over the entire struc-

| ❶ Spandau Citadel |  |

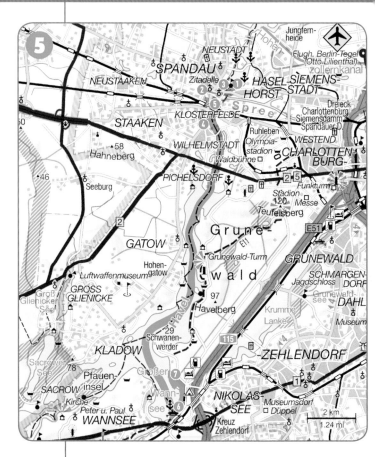

ture before walking along the walls of the fortress until you reach the "Unveiled" exhibition, which uses monuments taken from around Berlin to tell the story of the city. These include the INSIDER TIP head from the Lenin memorial that was dismantled in 1991, and whose removal was immortalised in the film "Goodbye Lenin".

01:00pm Bear right after leaving the citadel, then left after the bridge. In just a few minutes' walk you'll reach the ❷ **historic centre of Spandau**. The bijou houses lining the historic market square exude small-town charm, and give away the fact that Spandau was for many years an independent settlement that only became part of Berlin in

❷ historic centre of Spandau

1920. It's worth stopping on the way for lunch at the **❸ Brauhaus Spandau** *(Neuendorfer Str. 1 | www.brauhaus-spandau. de | Budget–Moderate)*, which serves rustic cuisine and also makes its own version of the Berlin speciality *Fassbrause.* For the best desserts, head south from the historic centre to the authentic and traditional **❹ Florida Eiscafé** *(Klosterstr. 15)*, which has over 50 flavours of ice cream.

02:30pm Once you've eaten your fill, **head to the ❺ Spandau-Lindenufer dock on the shores of the Havel next to the railway bridge.** A boat *(www.ms-heiterkeit.de)* departs from here at 2.30pm on the dot, heading towards Wannsee. As you float along the Havel, you can enjoy wonderful views of the Grunewald Tower (built in 1897–99 in honour of Kaiser Wilhelm I) and the island of Schwanenwerder, with its many villas. You will also catch a glimpse of the

White fleet: ships and swans on the Havel River

Strandbad Wannsee lido on the left just before the boat reaches its mooring.

03:45pm The boat now comes into dock on the **❻ Ronneby promenade**, where you have two options. If you haven't had enough of the Havel then you can simply stay on board and glide gently back to Spandau via the Glienicke bridge and the Pfaueninsel, arriving at 6pm. Alternatively, head for a refreshing dip at the **❼ Strandbad Wannsee about half an hour's walk along the riverbank to the north. If you'd rather avoid the walk then in summer you can also ride the S-Bahn for one stop to Nikolassee before taking the 312 bus to the Strandbad.** With its mile-long sandy beach and numerous deckchairs, this lido has served as Berlin's substitute for the Baltic coast for 110 years. Architecture aficionados will appreciate the yellow clinker-brick exterior of the resort buildings from the late 1920s, a prime example of the Neue Sachlichkeit (New Objectivity). Go for a swim, catch some rays, and if you fancy taking a turn in a rowing boat or pedalo afterwards then head to the **Wassersportcenter Berlin** (right next-door to the lido), where you can hire boats for 12–15 euros per hour. To head back into town, take the S7 from Nikolassee.

❸ Brauhaus Spandau

❹ Florida Eiscafé

❺ Spandau-Lindenufer

❻ Ronneby promenade

❼ Strandbad Wannsee

TRAVEL WITH KIDS

BONBONMACHEREI
(140–141 C–D2) *(Ø K3)*

How are sweets made? Kids can see how the mixture is prepared and also try them while still warm. Of course, you can also buy the drops packed up in little bags. Yummy! *Wed–Sat noon–7pm, closed July/ August and over Christmas/New Year | admission free | Mitte | Oranienburger Str. 32 | tel. 030 44 05 52 43 | www.bonbon macherei.de | S 1, 2, 25 Oranienburger Straße*

INSIDER TIP ► BVG CABRIOTOUR
(141 F2) *(Ø L3)*

A "ghost train" ride in the underground: during the summer season, a roofless carriage races through 35 km (22 miles) of dark tunnels in the underground system. Ready, set , helmets on – for the two hour tour starting at Alexanderplatz. *April–Oct Fri 7 and 10:20pm | tickets 50 euros, children 35 euros | tel. 030 25 62 52 56 | www. bvg.de | U/S Alexanderplatz*

CLIMB UP! (164 C2) *(Ø O)*

This high-ropes centre with 15 different courses is set in a forest on the edge of Berlin. Those with a head for heights can spend up to two and a half hours testing their fitness across a range of difficulty grades. The 180 m/590 ft zip line is a particular highlight, and there is also an extra route specially designed for small children aged three and above. No experience required. *April–Sept Tue– Sun (daily in the summer) 10am–7pm, March/Oct until 6pm | admission 19 euros incl.climbing kit | Henningsdorf | Ruppiner Chaussee 99 | www.climbup.de | S 25 Heiligensee*

KINDERBAD MONBIJOU
(141 D2) *(Ø K3)*

A lovely pool only for children with their parents or accompanying adult. The water is not deeper than 1.30 m (4 ft 3 in.) and parents quickly make contact with others at the water's edge. Nobody over the age of 15 is allowed in unless they are accompanied by a child. *June– Sept Mon–Fri 11am–7pm, Sat/Sun 10am– 7pm | admission 5.50 euros | Mitte | Oranienburger Str. 78 | tel. 030 2 82 86 52 | www.berlinerbaeder betriebe.de | S 1, 2, 25 Oranienburger Straße*

KOLLE 37 (147 D5) *(Ø L2)*

Exciting adventure playground very close to the Kollwitzplatz. Here children can run around wild, hammer on the

Children love big cities because there is so much to discover. And there is a great deal waiting for them in Berlin. Enjoy yourselves!

workbench or stroke the rabbits while adults can stroll around the district. *Mid-April–mid-Oct Mon–Fri noon–7pm, Sat 1–6pm, in winter Mon–Fri 11:30am–6pm, Sat 1–6pm | admission free | Prenzlauer Berg | Kollwitzstr. 37 | www.kolle37.de | U 2 Senefelderplatz*

KULTURPROJEKTE BERLIN

Most of the state museums have regular guided tours for children and workshops on the art on display. Just one example; in the Music Instrument Museum, the way instruments function is investigated playfully using the work "Peter and the Wolf" by Sergei Prokofiev. The staff have all studied art history or are trained teachers and have no difficulties in making young people really enthusiastic about museums. You can find out details of current events by phone. *Office: Mon–Fri 9am–4pm, Sat/Sun 9am–1pm | Mitte | Klosterstr. 68 | tel. 030 24 74 98 88 | www.kulturprojekte-berlin.de | U 2 Klosterstraße*

MACH MIT! MUSEUM
(147 E4) (*ℳ M2*)

Shelves you can climb on, soap shops, a crawling area – there are a lot of experiences in the Museum for children. There are workshops for handicrafts, pottery and acting. Exhibitions are also shown – on the Romans, for example. You can park your parents in the Family Café while you have fun! *Tue–Sun 10am–6pm | admission 5.50 euros; concessions 3.50 euros | Prenzlauer Berg | Senefelderstr. 5 | tel. 030 74 77 82 00 | www.machmitmuseum. de | S 41: Prenzlauer Allee*

THEATER AN DER PARKAUE
(165 E3) (*ℳ P4*)

State theatre for children and youngsters. "Peter and the Wolf" after Sergei Prokofiev is a hit with children from the age of five. "The Children's Transport – Berlin Kids on the Way to London" (from 12 y.) has even won prizes. *Lichtenberg | Parkaue 29 | tel. 030 5 57 75 20 | www.parkaue.de | S 41, 42 Frankfurter Allee*

FESTIVALS & EVENTS

Numerous events are real crowd-pullers. These include the "Long Night of the Museums" that is held twice a year and gets thousands up and about. Shuttle buses transport visitors from one museum to the next. The Karneval der Kulturen (Carnival of Cultures) sees visiting Brazilian samba dancers and Angolan drummers parading through Kreuzberg. And some of the attendees at the Green Week even arrive by tractor!

FESTIVALS/ EVENTS

JANUARY/FEBRUARY

Sechstagerennen (Six-day race): High-spirited bicycle race in the Velodrom; *Prenzlauer Berg | Landsberger Allee | tel. 030 44 30 44 30 | www.sechstagerennen-berlin.de*

Grüne Woche: Delicatessen specialities from all over the world at the Funkturm (Radio Tower); *Charlottenburg | info tel. 030 3 03 80 | www.gruenewoche.de*

FEBRUARY

⭐ ***Berlinale:*** International film festival; ten days of razzmatazz with German and international film stars and new cinema productions; *info tel. 030 25 92 00 | www.berlinale.de*

MARCH

Internationale Tourismusbörse (ITB): International Tourism Fair at the Funkturm; *Charlottenburg | tel. 030 3 03 80 | www.itb-berlin.de*

MAY/JUNE

Gallery Weekend: The city's galleries open their doors; *tel. 030 70 03 87 71 | www.gallery-weekend-berlin.de*

Theatertreffen Significant productions from Germany, Austria and Switzerland performed on Berlin's stages; *info tel. 030 25 48 90 | www.berlinerfestspiele.de/theatertreffen*

Internationale Luft- und Raumfahrtausstellung: Every two years, Schönefeld Airport is the place to be for all aviation enthusiasts (2020, 2022); *www.ila-berlin.de*

DFB Cup Final: Football festival in the Olympiastadium; *Charlottenburg | info tel. 030 8 96 99 40*

Lange Nacht der Wissenschaften: Presentation of work at research institutions; *www.langenachtderwissenschaften.de*

Karneval der Kulturen: Colourful, intercultural carnival procession on Whit Sunday; *www.karneval-der-kulturen.de*

Not only in summer is Berlin a city where people like to have a good time – the calendar is full of festivals of all kinds

JUNE/JULY

Christopher Street Day: Top event for gays and lesbians with a great parade from Ku'damm to Brandenburger Tor; *www.csd-berlin.de*

Classic Open Air on Gendarmenmarkt: Festive setting, catchy tunes; *Mitte | tel. 030 3 15 75 40 | www.classicopenair.de*

AUGUST

Long Night of the Museums: A visit to van Gogh & Co. in the evening; *info tel. 030 24 74 98 88 | www.lange-nacht-der-museen.de*

SEPTEMBER

Jüdische Kulturtage (Jewish Culture Days): Theatre performances, concerts and readings; *www.juedische-kulturtage.org*

Internationale Funkausstellung: Entertainment/electronics fair at the Funkturm; *Charlottenburg | b2c.ifa-berlin.de*

Berlin Marathon: More than 40,000 participants from all over the world start at Brandenburger Tor; *info tel. 030 30 12 88 10 | www.berlin-marathon.com*

Musikfest Berlin: three weeks of classical music of the highest standard; *www.berlinerfestspiele.de/musikfestberlin*

SEPTEMBER/OCTOBER

Internationales Literaturfestival: readings and more; *www.literaturfestival.com*

Festival of Lights: After nightfall, installations cast many of Berlin's sights in a new light for ten days; *festival-of-lights.de*

NOVEMBER

Jazzfest Berlin: An institution with international stars; *info tel. 030 25 48 91 00 | www.berlinerfestspiele.de/jazzfest*

DECEMBER

Weihnachtsmarkt am Gendarmenmarkt: Atmospheric Christmas market (one of several in the city) in a historical setting, offering artisan craftwork and concerts

LINKS, BLOGS, APPS & MORE

LINKS & BLOGS

www.berlin.de/international is Berlin's official internet site that offers comprehensive listings for hotels, entertainment, tickets for local events well as practical information about local authorities and online maps

www.visitberlin.de is an informative site with interesting offers for tourists to Berlin; including a list of events and travel tips for various age groups along with some useful listings for special interest groups like for example the environmentally aware

90erberlin.tumblr.com On this fascinating site, Michael Lange shows his black and white photos of Berlin in the 90s when it was full of empty spaces and construction sites – often directly next to a picture of the same place 20 years later

www.needleberlin.com Popular Berlin blog by Berlin writer Joseph Pearson. He writes about things like "How to get into the Berghain", but more often about serious, political topics.

www.exberliner.com Berlin's online English language magazine which includes listings for cultural events, reviews, general interest articles and a large classified section. The title is a play on expat

www.thewednesdaychef.com/berlin_on_a_platter/ an excellent and informative foodie blog written by the cookbook editor and award winning blogger Luisa Weiss. She writes about her "favourite bakeries and snack stands, hidden gems, gustatory wonders" and new restaurant discoveries

www.digitalinberlin.de is a site that is perfect for 'music lovers, adventures and individualists' with listings for music, movies, literature, interviews and free downloads

www.toytowngermany.com is the best online forum for expats in Germany and the topics of discussion include lo-

Regardless of whether you are still researching your trip or already in Berlin: these addresses will provide you with more information, videos and networks to make your holiday even more enjoyable.

cal news, reviews, relocation issues as well as legal and financial advice. The forum also organises a number of live social events via the site

www.iheartberlin.de Exciting Berlin blog with a calendar of upcoming events, a city guide and lots of interesting posts, e.g. about fashion or the inspiring people of Berlin

kreuzberged.com Beautiful blog with small, contemplative, often historical vignettes about Berlin, updated almost every day. From nostalgic pictures via poetic musings about trees to David Bowie's Berlin... it's all here.

VIDEOS & MUSIC

www.myvideo.de/Videos_A-Z?search Word=berlin if you search for "Berlin" on MyVideo you will not only find many TV series but also documentaries and whimsical short films

www.art-in-berlin.de/video.php Video documentary reports about current exhibitions and the corresponding artists

https://itunes.apple.com/us/podcast/berlin-stories-podcast/id302399493?mt=2 These podcasts are from the bi-weekly English radio broadcasts of 104.1 fm NPR Berlin. American and British writers read their reflections on Berlin and there also special editions with readings of passages from historical novels about Berlin

APPS

Fahrinfo Berlin Important accompaniment when travelling on Berlin's public transport: with a planner that shows you the fastest route from A to B. With the BVG smartphone app, you can buy a ticket (and the WelcomeCard, but no four-journey tickets) for all public transport (see also p. 131). The VBB app (from the Berlin-Brandenburg transport association) on the other hand offers four-journey tickets, but no WelcomeCard

Kultur Berlin Information about all types of concerts, theatres, exhibitions and cultural events. With admission prices, opening times and map of the event location

My Taxi Free app that connects to a taxi nearby; extremely reliable especially within the city centre. Only available for iPhones

TRAVEL TIPS

ARRIVAL

Most planes land and take off from *Tegel Airport* (142 C2) (*∅ D1*) in the north-west of the city. You can reach Bahnhof Zoo, the centre of the western part of the city, in about 20 min by taking the buses X9 and 109. To reach Alexanderplatz (in about 30 min, via Unter den Linden) take the express bus TXL. From *Schönefeld Airport* (www.berlin-airport.de) take the S 9 to Alexanderplatz (35 min) or to Bahnhof Zoo (50 min). A faster alternative is the airport express, a regional train that departs for the airport every half an hour. A taxi ride from Tegel to Bahnhof Zoo costs around 19 euros, to the Alexanderplatz approx. 25 euros, from Schönefeld into the city centre for approx. 35–40 euros. *Airport information (tel. 030 60 911150)*

RESPONSIBLE TRAVEL

While traveling you can influence a lot. Don't just keep track of your carbon footprint *(www.myclimate.org)* by planning an ecologically harmless route. Also think about how you can protect nature and culture abroad *(www.ecotrans.org)*. It is all the more important that as a tourist you take into consideration aspects such as the conservation of nature *(www.wwf.org)*, regional products, minimal use of cars, saving water and many more things. For more information on ecological Tourism look at *www.ecotourism.org*.

There are fast train connections from major European stations to Berlin-Spandau, Hauptbahnhof (main station) and Ostbahnhof. *Information: tel. 0800 150 70 90 | www.bahn.de*

The motorways to and from Berlin are good. However, there are often traffic jams on the A10 ring road. The centre within the inner district line ring is a "green zone"; only cars with a green sticker are allowed to drive here. *www.umwelt-plakette.de*

There are regular bus services several times a week from German and many foreign towns to Berlin. It is cheaper, but usually it takes longer than by train. Get an overview of the services at *www.fahrtenfuchs.de*. Berlin's Central Bus Station is located in Charlottenburg opposite the Funkturm. *Zentraler Omnibusbahnhof (ZOB)* (148 B5) (*∅ C5*) (*info tel. 030 35195 20 | www.iob-berlin.de*)

ADVANCE SALES

HEKticket (Hardenbergstr. 29d | tel. 030 2 30 99 30 | www.hekticket.de) sells tickets at half-price until shortly before performances begin. INSIDER TIP Tickets for museums are also available at reduced prices. *Showtime (tel. 030 80 60 29 29 | www.showtimetickets.de)* sell tickets in the KaDeWe department store; box office inside Friedrichstraße station: *Mon–Fri 8am–8pm, Sat 10am–6pm | Georgenstr. 14–18 | www.ber-ticket.de*

BANKS

Normal opening hours are 10am to 5pm

on weekdays; some banks however are open until 2pm on Saturdays.

BICYCLES, VELOTAXIS & SEGWAY

You can rent a bicycle from many bike shops and hotels in the city centre. The German Railway's (DB) "Call a Bike" *(www.callabike-interaktiv.de)* is very practical. The conspicuous DB bikes can be found at 150 different places in the heart of Berlin. They can be rented directly at a terminal, by telephone or app using your bank card or credit card. New clients have to register first. Fees are 8 cents/minute rising to a maximum of 15 euros/day. Another cheap alternative is Nextbike *(ww.nextbike.de,* various rental points).

You can also rent a *Biketaxi (tel. 030 93 95 83 46 | www.biketaxi.de)* from March to Oct and have somebody else do the hard work. A 60-minute tour with an individual route costs 45 euros. Or just stop an empty rickshaw on the street. The first kilometre costs 6 euros; after that, there is an hourly rate.

Yoove (tel. 030 6 52 15 73 97 | www.yoove. com) hires out Segways for 19.90 euros an hour; they can be collected at three different hire stations. Tours on Segways are also organised. You need a moped license and be at least 16 years old.

CITY TOURS

Bus no. 100 is terrific for those who like to get an overview on their own. It runs from Bahnhof Zoo to Alexanderplatz and is ideal for sightseeing – you pass most of the important attractions in the centre.

BUDGETING

Coffee	£1.80/$2.50– £3/$4	*for a cup of coffee*
Ice cream	£1.80/$2.50	*for two scoops of ice cream*
Döner	£2.20/$3–£3/$4.40	*for a döner kebab*
Museum	£3.50/$5–£10.50/$15	*state-run museums*
Bus	£2.39/$3.35	*for a one-way bus ticket*

BEROLINA SIGHTSEEING

City-Circle-Tour with 18 stops to hop on or off (daily 10am–6pm, in winter until 5pm, every 10 minutes in summer.) Day ticket 20 euros; two days 24 euros; start: Kurfürstendamm/Meinekestraße. *Info tel. 030 88 56 80 30 | www.berolina-berlin. com*

INSIDER TIP ROUTE 44

Migrant women guide visitors through the Neukölln district around Richardplatz. Those taking part find out how the women and girls live here. Incl. visit to a mosque. *Kulturbewegt e.V. | 5 euros | tel. 030 70 22 20 23 | www.route44-neukoelln.de*

SEGWAY TOUR

Yoove organises guided Segway tours starting from Potsdamer Platz for approx. 50 euros/person. *Tel. 030 6 52 15 73 97 | www.yoove.com*

SOLAR BOAT TOUR ◎

With the four-hour circular tour on the quiet solar boat you will see many places and buildings and save energy at the same time. Starting and finishing point: Urbanhafen in Kreuzberg. *Tel. 0151 54 22 80 44 | www.solarpolis.de*

CUSTOMS

EU citizens may import and export goods for their personal use tax-free. Duty-free for non-EU citizens are: 50g perfume, 2 l of wine, 1 l of spirits and 200 cigarettes.

EMBASSIES & CONSULATES

BRITISH EMBASSY
Wilhelmstr. 70/71 | 10117 Berlin | tel. 030 20457 0 | www.ukingermany.fco.gov.uk

EMBASSY OF THE UNITED STATES
Clayallee 170 | 14191 Berlin | tel. 030 83 05 0 | www.germany.usembassy.gov

EMBASSY OF CANADA
Leipziger Platz 17 | 10117 Berlin | tel. 030 20 312 0 | travel.gc.ca/assistance/embassies-consulates/germany

EMERGENCY SERVICES

On-call medical service: 030 31 00 31 | Fire brigade: tel. 112 | Police: tel. 110 | childrens' emergency service: tel. 030 61 00 61 | veterinarian emergency service: tel. 030 4 37 46 63 34 | on-call dentist: tel. 030 89 00 43 33

IMMIGRATION

No visa is necessary for EU citizens to travel to or work in Germany. Non-EU citizens require a visa (valid up to 90 days) – or a residence or settlement permit. More detailed, up-to-date information online, e.g. *www.workpermit.com/germany/employer1.htm*.

INFORMATION

BERLIN TOURISMUS & KONGRESS GMBH
Karlsbad 11 | 10785 Berlin | tel. 030 25 00 25 | www.visitberlin.de | hotline Mon–Fri 9am–7pm, Sat 10am–6pm, Sun 10am–2pm.
Branches:
– Mitte (Pariser Platz | Brandenburger Tor, south wing | April–Oct daily 9:30am–7pm, Nov–March until 6pm)
– Mitte (Panoramastr. 1a | in the TV tower | daily 10am–6pm, Nov–March until 4pm)
– Mitte (Europaplatz 1 | main railway station | daily 8am–10pm)
– Charlottenburg (Kurfürstendamm 1/corner Rankestraße) | April–Oct daily 10am–6pm, Nov–March until 4pm)

CURRENCY CONVERTER

£	€	€	£
1	1.14	1	0.88
3	3.43	3	2.63
5	5.70	5	4.38
13	14.85	13	11.38
40	46	40	35
75	86	75	66
120	137	120	105
250	286	250	219
500	571	500	438

$	€	€	$
1	0.81	1	1.23
3	2.43	3	3.70
5	4.05	5	6.17
13	10.54	13	16.04
40	32.42	40	49.35
75	61	75	92.52
120	97	120	148
250	203	250	308
500	405	500	617

For current exchange rates see www.xe.com

– Tegel Airport (Terminal A/Gate 2 | daily 8am–9pm)
– Schönefeld Airport (Terminal A, main hall | daily 8am–8pm)

PHONE & MOBILE PHONE

The dialling code for Germany is 0049, the area code for Berlin is (0)30. Dial 0044 for Great Britain followed by the area code without "0" and 001 for USA and Canada.

PUBLIC TRANSPORT

Most underground lines run around the clock on Fri and Sat. If there is no underground to where you are staying, night buses will bring you home. The district line usually runs until around 1am. There are three fare zones for suburban services. A and B cover the whole city; C also covers the surrounding area including Potsdam. Currently, a single ticket (A) costs 2.70 euros (concessions: 1.70 euros); day ticket 7 euros. *BVG Information: tel. 03019449 | www.bvg.de*. Families can travel economically with the *Welcome-Card*: For just 29.50 euros, the *WelcomeCard* voucher booklet allows you to discover Berlin and Potsdam three days long on the Berlin-Brandenburg public network. A max. of three children (under 15 years old) can travel on an adult ticket. The card is available under *www.visitberlin. de*, where tickets for the district line, BVG, and DB Regio are sold, as well as at the information centres and in many hotels.

TAXI

The basic fare is 3.40 euros, normal fare for distances of up to 7 km (less than 4½ miles) 1.79 euros/km; from 7 km, 1.28 euros/km. Short distances under 2 km (1¼ miles) that do not take longer than 10 minutes cost 4 euros/journey. These fares only apply to taxis that are flagged down, and you must ask for them. *www.taxi-in-berlin.de/taxitarif*

WEATHER IN BERLIN

	Jan	Feb	March	April	May	June	July	Aug	Sept	Oct	Nov	Dec
Daytime temperatures in °C/°F	2/36	3/37	8/46	13/55	19/66	22/72	24/75	23/73	19/66	13/55	7/45	3/37
Nighttime temperatures in °C/°F	−3/27	−3/27	0/32	4/39	8/46	12/54	14/57	13/55	10/50	6/43	2/36	−1/30
Sunshine hours/day	2	3	5	6	8	8	8	7	6	4	2	1
Precipitation days/month	11	9	8	9	9	9	11	9	8	9	10	9

Sunshine hours/day Precipitation days/month

USEFUL PHRASES GERMAN

PRONUNCIATION

We have provided a simple pronunciation aid for the german words
(see the square brackets). Note the following:

ch   usually like ch in Scottish "loch", shown here as [kh]
g   hard as in "get"
ß   is a double s
ä   like the vowel in "fair" or "bear"
ö   a little like er as in "her"
ü   is spoken as ee with rounded lips, like the French "tu"
ie   is ee as in "fee", but ei is like "height", shown here as [ei]
'   stress on the following syllable

IN BRIEF

Yes/No/Maybe	Ja [yah]/Nein [nein]/Vielleicht [fee'leikht]
Please/Thank you	Bitte ['bi-te]/Danke ['dan-ke]
Sorry	Entschuldige [ent'shul-di-ge]
Excuse me, please	Entschuldigen Sie [ent'shul-di-gen zee]
May I...?/ Pardon?	Darf ich...? [darf ikh]/Wie bitte? [vee 'bi-te]
I would like to.../ have you got...?	Ich möchte... [ikh 'merkh-te]/ Haben Sie...? ['hab-en zee]
How much is...?	Wie viel kostet...? [vee-feel 'koss-tet]
I (don't) like this	Das gefällt mir/nicht [das ge-'felt meer/nikht]
good/bad	gut/schlecht [goot/shlekht]
broken/doesn't work	kaputt [ka-'put]/funktioniert nicht/ funk-tsion-'eert nikht]
too much/much/little	(zu) viel/wenig [tsoo feel/'vay-nikh]
Help!/Attention!/ Caution!	Hilfe! ['hil-fe]/Achtung! [akh-'tung]/ Vorsicht! ['for-sikht]
ambulance	Krankenwagen ['kran-ken-vaa-gen]/ Notarzt ['note-aatst]
police/fire brigade	Polizei [pol-i-'tsei]/Feuerwehr ['foy-er-vayr]
danger/dangerous	Gefahr [ge-'far]/gefährlich [ge-'fair-likh]

GREETINGS, FAREWELL

Good morning!/afternoon!/evening!/night!	Gute(n) Morgen ['goo-ten 'mor-gen]/Tag [taag]/ Abend ['aa-bent]/Nacht [nakht]
Hello!/Goodbye!	Hallo ['ha-llo]/Auf Wiedersehen [owf 'vee-der-zayn]

Sprechen Sie Deutsch?

"Do you speak German?" This guide will help you to say the basic words and phrases in German.

See you!	Tschüss [chüss]
My name is...	Ich heiße... [ikh 'hei-sse]
What's your name?	Wie heißt Du [vee heist doo]/ heißen Sie? ['heiss-en zee]
I'm from...	Ich komme aus... [ikh 'ko-mme ows]

DATE & TIME

Monday/Tuesday	Montag ['moan-tag]/Dienstag ['deens-tag]
Wednesday/Thursday	Mittwoch ['mit-vokh]/Donnerstag ['don-ers-tag]
Friday/Saturday	Freitag ['frei-tag]/Samstag ['zams-tag]
Sunday/holiday	Sonntag ['zon-tag]/Feiertag ['fire-tag]
today/tomorrow/	heute ['hoy-te]/morgen ['mor-gen]/
yesterday	gestern ['gess-tern]
hour/minute	Stunde ['shtun-de]/Minute [min-'oo-te]
day/night/week	Tag [tag]/Nacht [nakht]/Woche ['vo-khe]
What time is it?	Wie viel Uhr ist es? ['vee-feel oor ist es]
It's three o'clock	Es ist drei Uhr [ez ist drei oor]

TRAVEL

open/closed	offen ['off-en]/geschlossen [ge-'shloss-en]
entrance (vehicles)	Zufahrt ['tsoo-faat]
entrance/exit	Eingang ['ein-gang]/Ausgang ['ows-gang]
arrival/arrival (flight)	Ankunft ['an-kunft]/Abflug ['ap-floog]
toilets/restrooms /	Toiletten [twa-'let-en]/
ladies/gentlemen	Damen ['daa-men]/Herren ['her-en]
(no) drinking water	(kein) Trinkwasser [(kein) 'trink-vass-er]
Where is...?/Where are...?	Wo ist...? [vo ist]/Wo sind...? [vo zint]
left/right	links [links]/rechts [rekhts]
straight ahead/back	geradeaus [ge-raa-de-'ows]/zurück [tsoo-'rük]
close/far	nah [naa]/weit [veit]
taxi/cab	Taxi ['tak-si]
bus stop/	Bushaltestelle [bus-hal-te-'shtell-e]/
cab stand	Taxistand ['tak-si- shtant]
parking lot/parking garage	Parkplatz ['park-plats]/Parkhaus ['park-hows]
street map/map	Stadtplan ['shtat-plan]/Landkarte ['lant-kaa-te]
airport/ train station	Flughafen ['floog-ha-fen]/ Bahnhof ['baan-hoaf]
schedule/ticket	Fahrplan ['faa-plan]/Fahrschein ['faa-shein]
I would like to rent...	Ich möchte... mieten [ikh 'mer-khte... 'mee-ten]
a car/a bicycle	ein Auto [ein 'ow-to]/ein Fahrrad [ein 'faa-raat]
a motorhome/RV	ein Wohnmobil [ein 'vone-mo-beel]
a boat	ein Boot [ein 'boat]

petrol/gas station	Tankstelle ['tank-shtell-e]
petrol/gas / diesel	Benzin [ben-'tseen]/Diesel ['dee-zel]
breakdown/repair shop	Panne ['pan-e]/Werkstatt ['verk-shtat]

FOOD & DRINK

Could you please book a table for tonight for four?	Reservieren Sie uns bitte für heute Abend einen Tisch für vier Personen [rez-er-'vee-ren zee uns 'bi-te für 'hoy-te 'aa-bent 'ein-en tish für feer pair-'zo-nen]
The menu, please	Die Speisekarte, bitte [dee 'shpei-ze-kaa-te 'bi-te]
Could I please have...?	Könnte ich... haben? ['kern-te ihk... 'haa-ben]
with/without ice/	mit [mit]/ohne Eis ['oh-ne eis]/
sparkling	Kohlensäure ['koh-len-zoy-re]
vegetarian/allergy	Vegetarier(in) [veg-e-'taa-ree-er]/Allergie [al-air-'gee]
May I have the bill, lease?	Ich möchte zahlen, bitte [ikh 'merkh-te 'tsaa-len 'bi-te]

SHOPPING

Where can I find...?	Wo finde ich...? [vo 'fin-de ikh]
I'd like.../I'm looking for...	Ich möchte... [ikh 'merkh-te]/Ich suche... [ikh 'zoo-khe]
pharmacy/chemist	Apotheke [a-po-'tay-ke]/Drogerie [dro-ge-'ree]
shopping centre	Einkaufszentrum [ein-kowfs-'tsen-trum]
expensive/cheap/price	teuer ['toy-er]/billig ['bil-ig]/Preis [preis]
more/less	mehr [mayr]/weniger ['vay-ni-ger]
organically grown	aus biologischem Anbau [ows bee-o-'lo-gish-em 'an-bow]

WHERE TO STAY

I have booked a room	Ich habe ein Zimmer reserviert [ikh 'haa-be ein 'tsi-mer rez-erv-'eert]
Do you have any... left?	Haben Sie noch ein... ['haa-ben zee nokh]
single room	Einzelzimmer ['ein-tsel-tsi-mer]
double room	Doppelzimmer ['dop-el-tsi-mer]
breakfast/half board	Frühstück ['frü-shtük]/Halbpension ['halp-pen-si-ohn]
full board	Vollpension ['foll-pen-si-ohn]
shower/sit-down bath	Dusche ['doo-she]/Bad [baat]
balcony/terrace	Balkon [bal-'kohn]/Terrasse [te-'rass-e]
key/room card	Schlüssel ['shlü-sel]/Zimmerkarte ['tsi-mer-kaa-te]
luggage/suitcase	Gepäck [ge-'pek]/Koffer ['koff-er]/Tasche ['ta-she]

BANKS, MONEY & CREDIT CARDS

bank/ATM	Bank/Geldautomat [bank/'gelt-ow-to-maat]
pin code	Geheimzahl [ge-'heim-tsaal]
I'd like to change... euros	Ich möchte... Euro wechseln [ikh 'merkh-te... 'oy-ro 'vek-seln]

cash/credit card	bar [bar]/Kreditkarte [kre-'dit-kaa-te]
bill/coin	Banknote ['bank-noh-te]/Münze ['mün-tse]

HEALTH

doctor/dentist/	Arzt [aatst]/Zahnarzt ['tsaan-aatst]/
paediatrician	Kinderarzt ['kin-der-aatst]
hospital/	Krankenhaus ['kran-ken-hows]/
emergency clinic	Notfallpraxis ['note-fal-prak-sis]
fever/pain	Fieber ['fee-ber]/Schmerzen ['shmer-tsen]
diarrhoea/nausea	Durchfall ['doorkh-fal]/Übelkeit ['ü-bel-keit]
inflamed/injured	entzündet [ent-'tsün-det]/verletzt [fer-'letst]
prescription	Rezept [re-'tsept]
pain reliever/tablet	Schmerzmittel ['shmerts-mit-el]/Tablette [ta-'blet-e]

POST, TELECOMMUNICATIONS & MEDIA

stamp/letter	Briefmarke ['brief-maa-ke]/Brief [brief]
postcard	Postkarte ['posst-kaa-te]
I'm looking for a prepaid	Ich suche eine Prepaid-Karte für mein Handy [ikh
card for my mobile	'zoo-khe 'ei-ne 'pre-paid-kaa-te für mein 'hen-dee]
Do I need a special	Brauche ich eine spezielle Vorwahl?
area code?	['brow-khe ikh 'ei-ne shpets-ee-'ell-e 'fore-vaal]
Where can I find internet	Wo finde ich einen Internetzugang?
access?	[vo 'fin-de ikh 'ei-nen 'in-ter-net-tsoo-gang]
socket/adapter/	Steckdose ['shtek-doh-ze]/Adapter [a-'dap-te]/
charger/wi-fi	Ladegerät ['laa-de-ge-rayt]/WLAN ['vay-laan]

LEISURE, SPORTS & BEACH

bike/scooter rental	Fahrrad-['faa-raat]/Mofa-Verleih ['mo-fa fer-lei]
rental shop	Vermietladen [fer-'meet-laa-den]
lesson	Übungsstunde ['ü-bungs-shtun-de]

NUMBERS

0 null [null]	10 zehn [tsayn]	20 zwanzig ['tsvantsikh]
1 eins [eins]	11 elf [elf]	50 Fünfzig ['fünf-tsikh]
2 zwei [tsvei]	12 zwölf [tsvölf]	100 (ein) Hundert ['hun-dert]
3 drei [drei]	13 dreizehn [' dreitsayn]	200 Zwei Hundert [tsvei 'hun-dert]
4 vier [feer]	14 vierzehn ['feertsayn]	1000 (ein) Tausend ['tow-zent]
5 fünf [fünf]	15 fünfzehn ['fünftsayn]	2000 Zwei Tausend [tsvei 'tow-zent]
6 sechs [zex]	16 sechzehn ['zekhtsayn]	10 000 Zehn Tausend [tsayn 'tow-zent]
7 sieben ['zeeben]	17 siebzehn ['zeebtsayn]	
8 acht [akht]	18 achtzehn ['akhtsayn]	½ ein halb [ein halp]
9 neun [noyn]	19 neunzehn ['noyntsayn]	¼ ein viertel [ein 'feer-tel]

STREET ATLAS

The green line indicates the Discovery Tour "Berlin at a glance"
The blue line indicates the other Discovery Tours
All tours are also marked in the pull-out map

Exploring Berlin

The map on the back cover shows how the area has been sub-divided

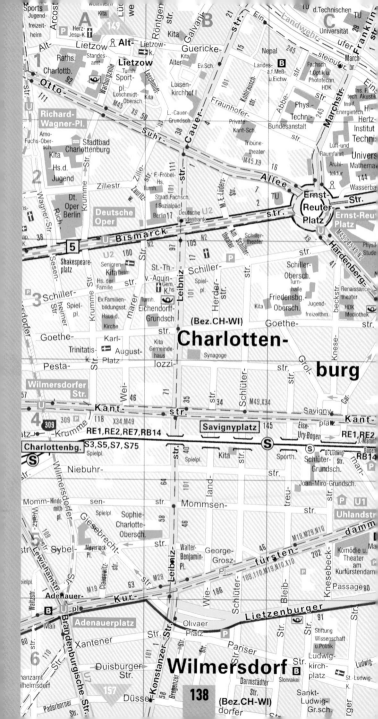

Charlotten-burg

Wilmersdorf

(Bez.CH-WI)

138

(Bez.CH-WI)

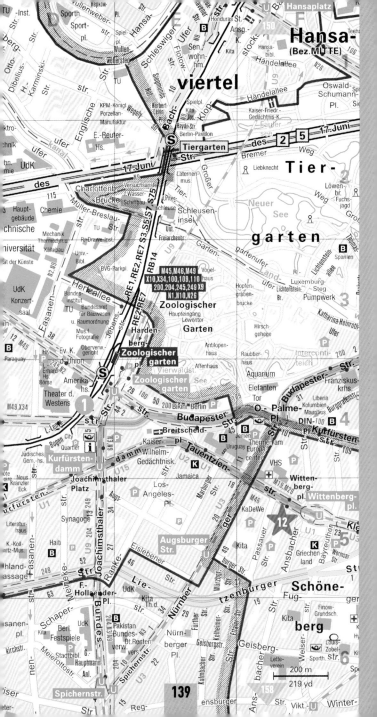

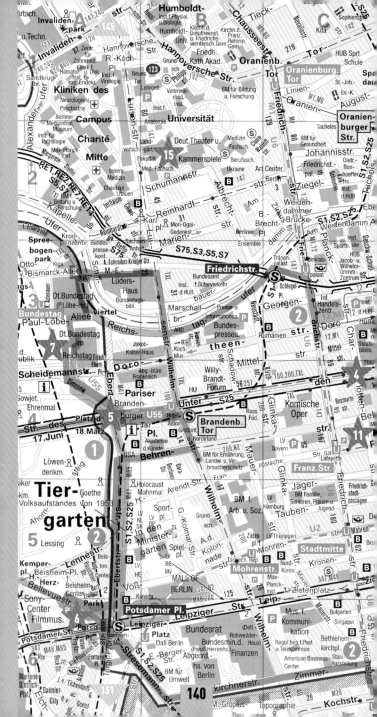

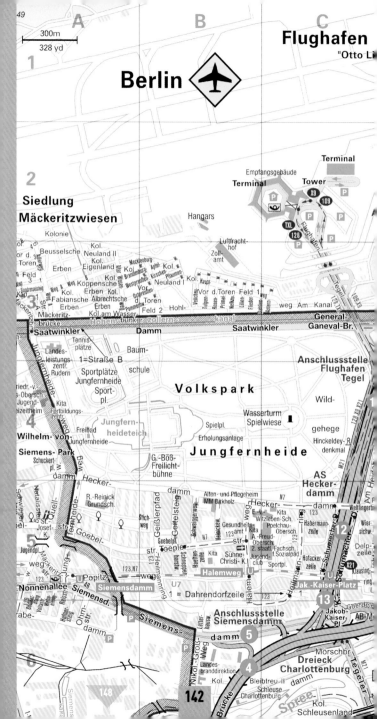

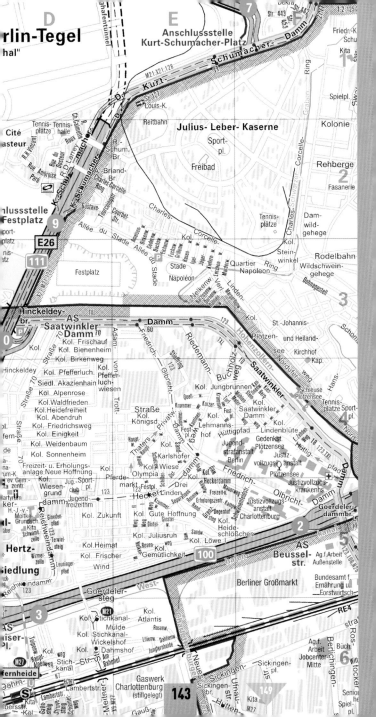

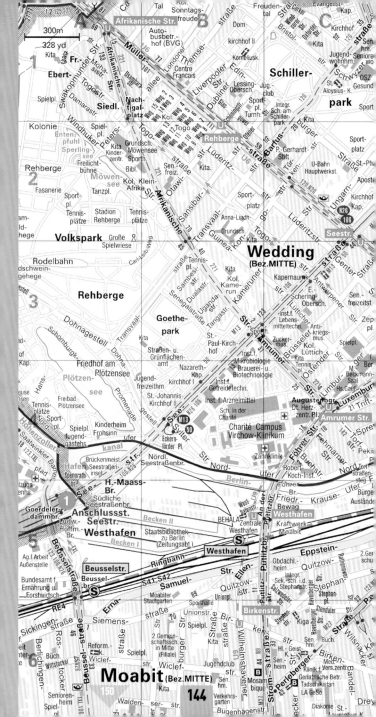

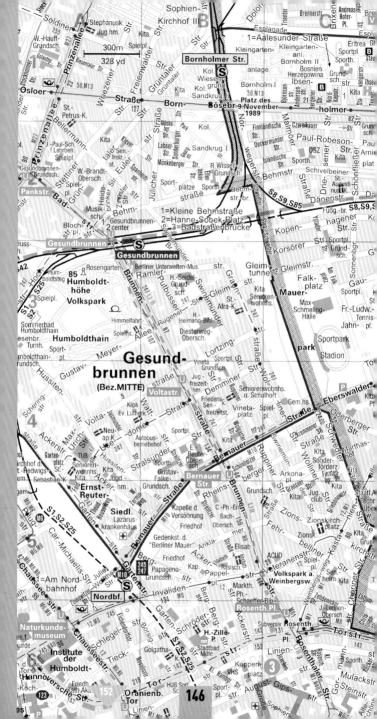

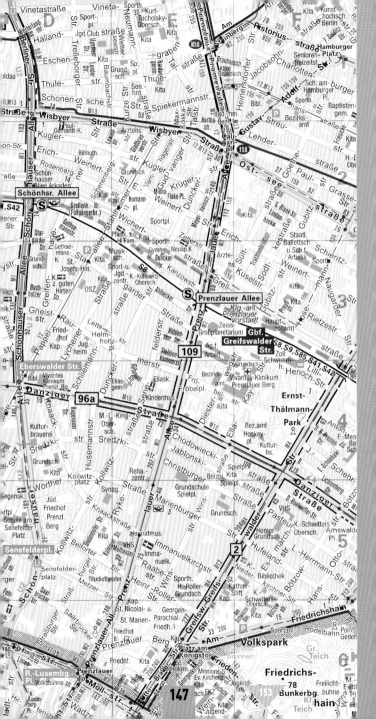

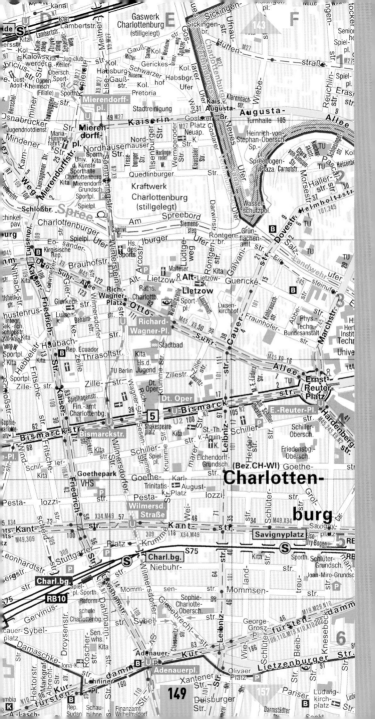

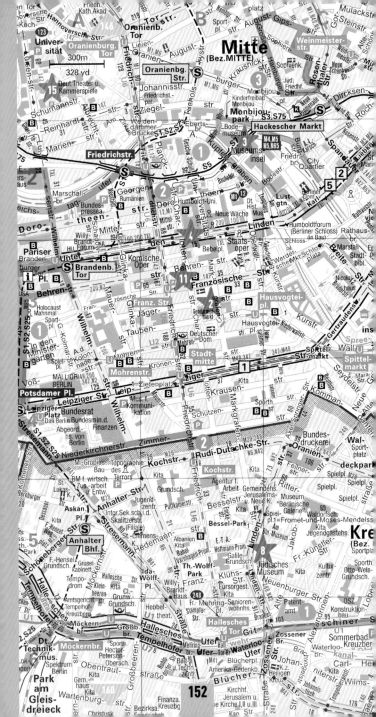

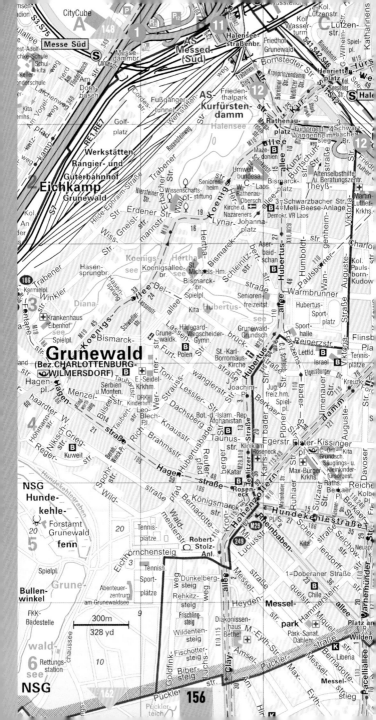

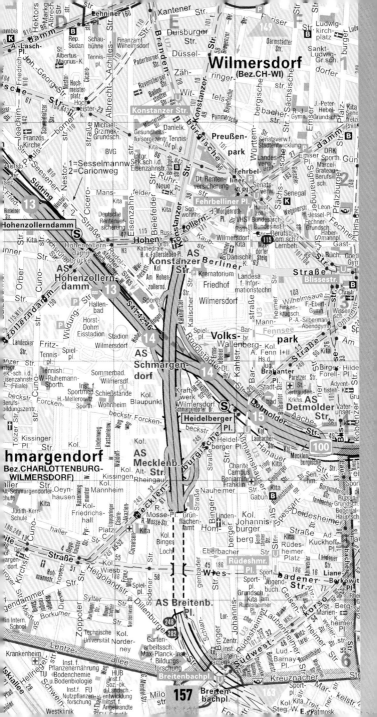

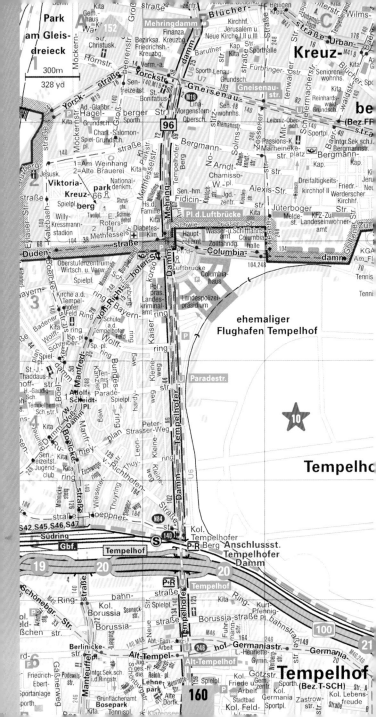

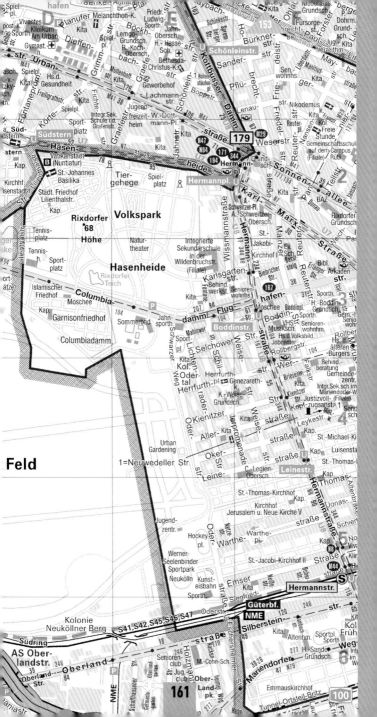

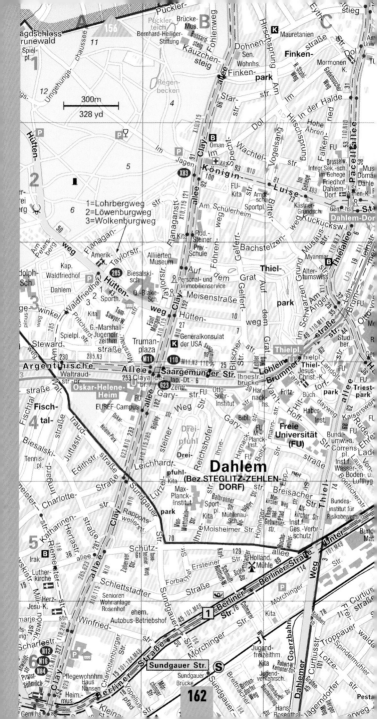

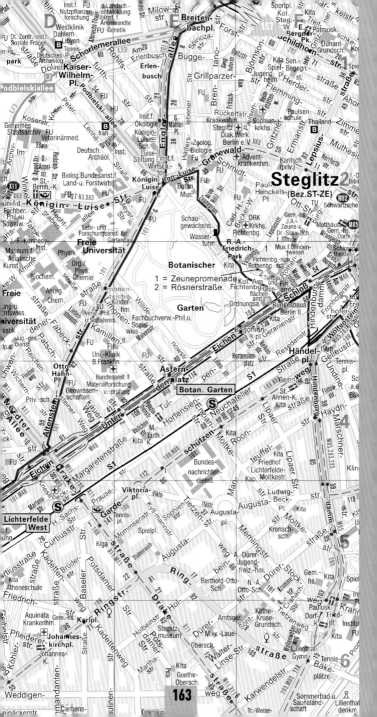

Steglitz
(Bez.ST-ZE)

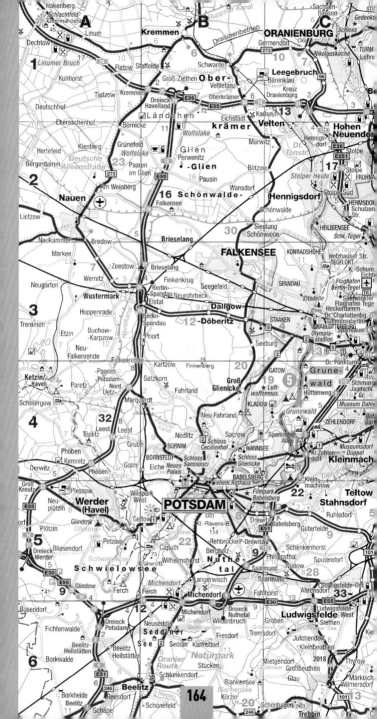

This index lists a selection of the streets and squares shown in the street atlas.

KEY TO STREET ATLAS

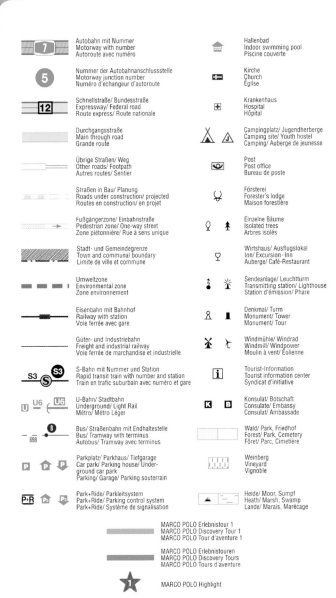

7	Autobahn mit Nummer / Motorway with number / Autoroute avec numéro
5	Nummer der Autobahnanschlussstelle / Motorway junction number / Numéro d'echangeur d'autoroute
12	Schnellstraße/ Bundesstraße / Expressway/ Federal road / Route express/ Route nationale
	Durchgangsstraße / Main through road / Grande route
	Übrige Straßen/ Weg / Other roads/ Footpath / Autres routes/ Sentier
	Straßen in Bau/ Planung / Roads under construction/ projected / Routes en construction/ en projet
	Fußgängerzone/ Einbahnstraße / Pedestrian zone/ One-way street / Zone piétonnière/ Rue à sens unique
	Stadt- und Gemeindegrenze / Town and communal boundary / Limite de ville et commune
	Umweltzone / Environmental zone / Zone environnement
	Eisenbahn mit Bahnhof / Railway with station / Voie ferrée avec gare
	Güter- und Industriebahn / Freight and industrial railway / Voie ferrée de marchandise et industrielle
S3	S-Bahn mit Nummer und Station / Rapid transit train with number and station / Train en trafic suburbain avec numéro et gare
U6	U-Bahn/ Stadtbahn / Underground/ Light Rail / Métro/ Métro Léger
8 **698**	Bus/ Straßenbahn mit Endhaltestelle / Bus/ Tramway with terminus / Autobus/ Tramway avec terminus
P	Parkplatz/ Parkhaus/ Tiefgarage / Car park/ Parking house/ Underground car park / Parking/ Garage/ Parking souterrain
P+R	Park+Ride/ Parkleitsystem / Park+Ride/ Parking control system / Park+Ride/ Système de signalisation

	Hallenbad / Indoor swimming pool / Piscine couverte
	Kirche / Church / Église
	Krankenhaus / Hospital / Hôpital
	Campingplatz/ Jugendherberge / Camping site/ Youth hostel / Camping/ Auberge de jeunesse
	Post / Post office / Bureau de poste
	Försterei / Forester's lodge / Maison forestière
	Einzelne Bäume / Isolated trees / Arbres isolés
	Wirtshaus/ Ausflugslokal / Inn/ Excursion- Inn / Auberge/ Café-Restaurant
	Sendeanlage/ Leuchtturm / Transmitting station/ Lighthouse / Station d'émission/ Phare
	Denkmal/ Turm / Monument/ Tower / Monument/ Tour
	Windmühle/ Windrad / Windmill/ Windpower / Moulin à vent/ Éolienne
i	Tourist-Information / Tourist information center / Syndicat d'initiative
K **B**	Konsulat/ Botschaft / Consulate/ Embassy / Consulat/ Ambassade
	Wald/ Park, Friedhof / Forest/ Park, Cemetery / Fôret/ Parc, Cimetière
	Weinberg / Vineyard / Vignoble
	Heide/ Moor, Sumpf / Heath/ Marsh, Swamp / Lande/ Marais, Marécage

MARCO POLO Erlebnistour 1 / MARCO POLO Discovery Tour 1 / MARCO POLO Tour d'aventure 1

MARCO POLO Erlebnistouren / MARCO POLO Discovery Tours / MARCO POLO Tours d'aventure

MARCO POLO Highlight

MARCO POLO TRAVEL GUIDES

The travel guides with
Insider
Tips

INDEX

This index lists all sights, museums and places, plus the names of important people featured in this guide. Numbers in bold indicate a main entry.

CREDITS

WRITE TO US

e-mail: info@marcopologuides.co.uk

Did you have a great holiday?
Is there something on your mind?
Whatever it is, let us know!
Whether you want to praise, alert us to errors or give us a personal tip – MARCO POLO would be pleased to hear from you.
We do everything we can to provide the very latest information for your trip.

Nevertheless, despite all of our authors' thorough research, errors can creep in. MARCO POLO does not accept any liability for this. Please contact us by e-mail or post.

MARCO POLO Travel Publishing Ltd
Pinewood, Chineham Business Park
Crockford Lane, Chineham
Basingstoke, Hampshire RG24 8AL
United Kingdom

PICTURE CREDITS
Cover photograph: Brandenburger Tor with balloons (Getty Images: S. Layda)
Photographs: Corbis/Demotix: S. Struck (20/21); DuMont Bildarchiv: Freyer (72 right), Specht (5, 10, 76/77, 122, 125); R. Freyer (66, 72 left, 92, 122/123, 123, 124, 124/125, 126 top); S. Layda (1), Nikada (4 top, 12/13), querbeet (23); J. Gläser (69); huber-images: M. Borchi (39), G. Cozzi (45), L. Da Ros (26/27), M. Rellini (40, 136/137), R. Schmid (50); G. Knoll (75); Laif: A. Akhtar (64/65, 70), A. Back (9), H. Champollion (8), M. Danner (84, 104), T. Gerber (121), K. Harms (25), M. Jaeger (11), Th. Kierok (30), G. Knechtel (19 top), D. Schwelle (2, 14, 17, 18 top, 18 bottom, 36/37, 48, 59, 88), Wernet (117), G. Westrich (flap right, 7, 60), Laif/Gamma-Rapho/Hoa-Qui: S. Grandadam (95); Laif/hemis.fr: F. Guiziou (112); Laif/Le Figaro Magazine: Martin (4 bottom, 86/87); Laif/Zenit: Boening (98/99); Look: K. Johaentges (57); Look/age fotostock (55); mauritius images: W. Bibikow (52, 100), mauritius images/Alamy (42, 63, 81, 82, 126 bottom); mauritius images/imagebroker: Henkelmann (127), Reister (34), I. Schulz (103), L. Steiner (6), E. Wrba (46/47); picture-alliance/dpa (18 centre); picture-alliance/Eventpress Hoensch (97); picture-alliance/ZB (91); Smiling Berlin Verlag: Lasse Walter (19 bottom); Visum: M. Hanke (106/107), A. Kohls (flap left); M. Weigt (73, 78)

4th Edition – fully revised and updated 2019
Worldwide Distribution: Marco Polo Travel Publishing Ltd, Pinewood, Chineham Business Park, Crockford Lane, Basingstoke, Hampshire RG24 8AL, United Kingdom. Email: sales@marcopolouk.com
© MAIRDUMONT GmbH & Co. KG, Ostfildern
Chief editor: Marion Zorn; Author: Christine Berger, Editor: Juliane Wiedemeier
Programme supervision: Jochen Schürmann; Verlagsredaktion: Stephan Dürr, Lucas Forst-Gill, Susanne Heimburger, Nikolai Michaelis, Martin Silbermann, Kristin Wittemann
Picture editors: Gabriele Forst, Anja Schlatterer; What's hot: wunder media, Munich; Cartography street atlas: © MAIRDUMONT, Ostfildern; Cartography pull-out map: © MAIRDUMONT, Ostfildern; Design front cover, p. 1, pull-out map cover: Karl Anders – Büro für Visual Stories, Hamburg; interior: milchhof:atelier, Berlin; Discovery Tours, p. 2/3: Susan Chaaban Dipl.-Des. (FH)
Translated from the German by Susan Jones; Jozef van der Voort
Prepress: writehouse, Cologne; InterMedia, Ratingen
Phrase book in cooperation with Ernst Klett Sprachen GmbH, Stuttgart, Editorial by Pons Wörterbücher

DOS & DON'TS ✋

A few things you should avoid

DON'T FALL FOR STREET GAMBLERS

Groups of men – often from Eastern Europe – delude unsuspecting people into thinking that it is the easiest thing in the world to win at a game of "thimbles". Three matchboxes, cups or other objects – one of which has a bead, pea or ball hidden under it – are moved back and forth at great speed and the player has to guess where the ball is. Standard bets of 50 euros are taken – and there is a dead certainty that you will lose. Don't be fooled by other players who seem to be winning; they are all members of the gang.

DON'T DRIVE INTO THE CITY

Anybody who doesn't have four big suitcases, ten shopping bags and three poodles to drag through the city can easily do without a car. A lack of knowledge about the city, traffic jams and the lack of – or extremely expensive – parking spaces can quickly take all the fun out of your holiday. If you want to get around Berlin independently and flexibly, the reliable underground, district line, tram and bus networks will prove to be ideal.

DON'T BUY SMUGGLED CIGARETTES

Berlin is a great place for bargain-hunter: however, a packet of cigarettes bought at half price from a Vietnamese dealer is not really a good deal. These are illegally smuggled goods and buyers can also be punished by law.

DON'T DODGE FARES

Never forget to stamp your ticket! Berlin ticket inspectors like their job: they are inconspicuous in their everyday clothes and extremely diligent and merciless when they catch a fare-dodger in the underground or anywhere else. If you're caught, you will have to pay 60 euros! The best thing is to buy a weekly ticket or use a *Welcome Card* (see *Travel Tips, p. 131*).

DON'T TRAVEL BY TAXI WITHOUT A MAP

Be prepared that not all taxi drivers know the city or individual districts like the back of their hand. Passengers often have to tell taxi drivers where to go – especially in the more outlying areas. The best thing to do is to check the route on your map before you get into a taxi.

DON'T LEAVE YOUR BAGS UNATTENDED

Unfortunately, Berlin is a lucrative spot for pickpockets. The expert criminals make a big haul in stations, on escalators and in the hustle-and-bustle at large events. It is a good idea not to keep your wallet or purse in your hip or coat pocket, and always keep an eye on your handbag.

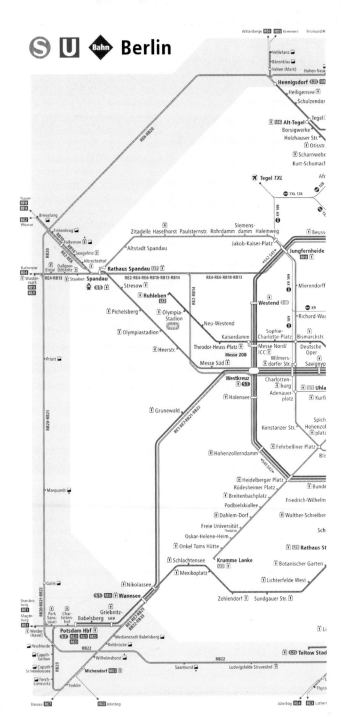